Men-at-Arms • 380

German Army Elite Units 1939–45

Gordon Williamson · Illustrated by Ramiro Bujeiro

Series editor Martin Windrow

First published in Great Britain in 2002 by Osprey Publishing,
Midland House, West Way, Botley, Oxford OX2 0PH, UK
44-02 23rd St, Suite 219, Long Island City, NY 11101, USA
E-mail: info@ospreypublishing.com

Transferred to digital print on demand 2009

First published 2002
7th impression 2008

Printed and bound by Cadmus Communications, USA

A CIP catalogue record for this book is available from the British Library

ISBN: 978 1 84176 405 4

Editorial by Martin Windrow
Design by Alan Hamp
Index by Alan Rutter
Origination by Magnet Harlequin, Uxbridge, UK
Typeset in Helvetica Neue and ITC New Baskerville

Artist's Note

Readers may care to note that the original paintings from which the colour plates in this book were prepared are available for private
sale. All reproduction copyright whatsoever is retained by the Publisher. All enquiries should be addressed to:

Ramiro Bujeiro, CC 28, 1602 Florida, Argentina

The Publishers regret that they can enter into not correspondence upon this matter.

FOR A CATALOGUE OF ALL BOOKS PUBLISHED BY OSPREY
MILITARY AND AVIATION PLEASE CONTACT:

Osprey Direct, c/o Random House Distribution Center,
400 Hahn Road, Westminster, MD 21157
Email: uscustomerservice@ospreypublishing.com

Osprey Direct, The Book Service Ltd, Distribution Centre,
Colchester Road, Frating Green, Colchester, Essex, CO7 7DW
E-mail: customerservice@ospreypublishing.com

www.ospreypublishing.com

GERMAN ARMY ELITE UNITS 1939–45

INTRODUCTION

Hauptmann Bernhard Klemz, commander of 5 Kompanie, Panzer-Regiment 'Grossdeutschland', in the regulation field-grey service uniform worn by armoured personnel when on leave or service away from their armoured vehicles. Note that he is not wearing the 'GD' ciphers on his shoulder straps; photographs showing soldiers failing to wear the special unit insignia to which they were entitled are not uncommon.

THE GERMAN ARMY was no different from any other army in the world in having a number of units which were considered 'élite'. Some of these were units or formations which, after unremarkable beginnings, established themselves as élite through their performance on the battlefield. Others were considered élite from the moment of their creation, having been formed around cadre elements from other units which had already earned that reputation. In some cases entire arms of service (e.g. the Luftwaffe's paratroopers) were considered to belong to an élite due to the extremely high selection standards and procedures that they enforced.

The formations and units covered in this work represent a selection and should in no way be considered exhaustive. Those included have been chosen, in the main, because they were granted some form of visible distinction which indicated that there was something 'special' about them, whether it be a cuffband, shoulder strap emblem, piping colour to their uniform, or unofficial unit insignia. However, such visible distinctions alone were not in themselves an indication of truly élite status: not every unit granted such insignia could be considered outstanding on the battlefield. On the other hand, as a general rule the majority of truly élite units were either granted, or unofficially adopted, some form of distinguishing insignia. In the final analysis the truly élite units – those whose record will live on in the annals of military history – were those that distinguished themselves by deeds of gallantry and sacrifice on the field of battle.

'GROSSDEUTSCHLAND'

This, the premier formation of the German Army, had its origins in the Berlin Guard detachment. In 1936 Generaloberst von Fritsch, Commander-in-Chief of the Army, had decreed that every unit of the army should send its best-drilled soldiers on rotation for service on ceremonial duties with the Guard in the capital city. The unit soon gained a reputation for the smartness of its drill and its immaculate turn-out. Expanded to regimental size in June 1937, it was formally titled Wachregiment Berlin and given the right to wear a distinctive 'W' cipher on its shoulder straps.

In April 1939, in reflection of the fact that its soldiers were drawn not from a specific local region as with most army units but was made up of the best from throughout the entire Reich, the regiment was renamed Infanterie-Regiment 'Grossdeutschland' ('Great Germany'). From being a predominantly ceremonial unit the regiment, to which a draft from the Infanterie-Lehr-Regiment demonstration unit was added in October 1939, was to become a superbly trained combat-ready infantry unit.

Still working up on the outbreak of war, 'Grossdeutschland' did not take part in the Polish campaign, although an offshoot from the regiment which was formed into a personal escort unit for Adolf Hitler under the title Führer-Begleit-Bataillon did see non-combat service in Poland.

The first significant action for the new regiment came during the 1940 campaign in the West, where it took part in the march through Belgium and into France, seeing combat against both French and British troops. It was to be no easy baptism of fire and 'Grossdeutschland' was involved in severe fighting on several occasions. After the fall of France, 'Grossdeutschland' remained on occupation duty while being reorganised and expanded to the strength of a regimental combat group. In April 1941 it took part in the invasion of Yugoslavia and was involved in the capture of Belgrade where it seized the radio station, reopening it as a German military station. By June, 'Grossdeutschland' had moved into reserve near Warsaw as Germany prepared for her invasion of the Soviet Union.

When Operation 'Barbarossa' began, elements of 'Grossdeutschland' crossed the River Bug in support of 7. Panzer-Division, taking part in the encirclement and capture of Minsk before pushing on to the Dnieper. They continued north-east in the general direction of Moscow, reaching Yelnya before being abruptly shifted south, where the formation engaged the Red Army in fierce fighting around Konotop, Putivi and Romny to the east of Kiev. The regiment was then diverted northwards once again, eventually being allowed some rest and recuperation around Orel. By the end of 1941 the regiment was lying to the south of the River Oka in defensive positions confronting the Soviet counter-attack before Moscow. Its first year in Russia had cost 'Grossdeutschland' over 4,000 killed or wounded, but had earned it a first-class reputation. The early part of 1942 was spent in defensive actions against Red Army units and offensive sweeps against heavily armed partisans.

'Grossdeutschland''s performance had been impressive enough for the decision to be taken to expand it yet again, this time to divisional status, and reorganisation began in April 1942. The formation was officially redesignated as Infanterie-Division (mot) 'Grossdeutschland' on 17 April 1942, and was allocated its own Panzer battalion. From its

ABOVE LEFT **A young tank crewman from Panzer-Regiment 'Grossdeutschland' poses proudly for a portrait photograph in his black vehicle uniform; normally a grey rather than a white shirt would be worn. Note the 'GD' ciphers on his shoulder straps, embroidered in rose-pink thread on the black wool strap.**

ABOVE **Leutnant 'Diddo' Diddens of Sturmgeschütz-Abteilung 'Grossdeutschland'. He wears the standard third-pattern Sütterlin script cuffband on the right sleeve, and the officer's gilt metal 'GD' ciphers on his shoulder straps.**

OPPOSITE **'Grossdeutschland' shoulder straps: (Left) Mid-war type in field-grey wool for the rank of Unterfeldwebel. (2nd, 3rd & 4th left) Early dark green wool straps for Feldwebel, Oberfeldwebel and Stabs-feldwebel. (2nd right & right) Officers' straps for Leutnant and Oberleutnant. All the NCO examples have white metal ciphers and the officer examples gilt metal ciphers.**

'*Grossdeutschland*' cuffbands –
from top to bottom:
First pattern, machine-woven
in aluminium thread Gothic
script on dark green rayon.
Third pattern, hand-embroidered
in aluminium wire Sütterlin
script on black doeskin.
Fourth pattern, machine-
embroidered in silver-grey
yarn on black wool.
Fifth pattern, machine-
embroidered in 'copperplate'
script on black wool.

form-up point at Ryetachiza the division attacked eastwards towards Kursk in late June 1942, getting as far as Voronezh on 6 July before turning south and fighting its way to the junction of the Rivers Don and Donetz north-east of Rostov by the end of that month.

On 1 August the division moved into reserve, based at Smolensk. Within a week of reaching Smolensk it was on the move again, however, pushing northwards to engage the enemy at Rzhev from early September through to October. It was here that 'Grossdeutschland' saw some of its heaviest fighting of the entire war, and in dreadful conditions; the autumn rains had turned the landscape into something akin to the muddy battlefields of France in the Great War. The fighting in this area, and especially in the hellish Lutschessa Valley, cost the division over 12,000 men.

In early 1943 the division was involved in the unsuccessful attempts to defend Kharkov and held back the Red Army long enough for the predominantly Waffen-SS units in the city to evacuate. Whilst in a rest area near Poltava the division received its own integral detachment of PzKw VI Tiger heavy tanks – a clear mark of its élite status, since these tanks were almost invariably limited to independent units under Corps or Army control. The division then took part in the counter-attack towards Kharkov, capturing Tomarovka before being pulled out of the line for rest and refitting. On 23 June 1943 the division was redesignated once again, now being entitled Panzergrenadier-Division 'Grossdeutschland'.

The division took part in the early stages of Operation 'Citadel', the armoured offensive at Kursk, and made good progress against stiff opposition before once again being pulled out of the line on 18 July. This was to be the beginning of a long period of employment as a 'fire brigade' for the Eastern Front, rushed from crisis point to crisis point; the arrival of this seasoned and very powerful formation would often be sufficient to prevent an enemy breakthrough, though once again at a terrible cost in casualties. By this point many of the veterans who had started the war with the GD had fallen, yet the ésprit de corps of the German Army's premier combat formation never faltered.

The first half of 1944 was spent in furious defensive battles, though on a few rare occasions the division was able to go onto the attack. 'Grossdeutschland' distinguished itself yet again at the see-sawing battles around Targul Frumos, first defending then counter-attacking, then defending yet again. In the summer it was pulled out of the line again for a brief period of rest and refitting; and during this period the 'Grossdeutschland' elements serving with the Guard Battalion in Berlin were instrumental in putting down the attempted *putsch* following the abortive attempt to assassinate Hitler on 20 July. Thereafter the Guard Battalion was increased to regimental status as the

Wachregiment. The summer of 1944 also saw elements of the divisional Panzer-Regiment, in France for refitting with the PzKw V Panther tank, sent into action against the Allies following the Normandy landings.

In November 1944 the Panzer-Korps 'Grossdeutschland' was created, comprising Panzergrenadier-Division 'Grossdeutschland' and Panzergrenadier-Division 'Brandenburg'. By late 1944 the GD division was in action on the northern sector of the Eastern Front, defending the area around the Baltic port of Memel. 'Grossdeutschland' had been weakened not only by combat losses but by providing the cadres for new formations such as the Führer-Begleit-Division, the Führer-Grenadier-Division and Panzergrenadier-Division 'Kurmark'. It spent the remaining few months of the war in desperate defensive actions in East Prussia, though some elements were successfully evacuated by sea to Schleswig Holstein and avoided capture by the Soviets. The Wachregiment was destroyed in the final battles for Berlin.

Main elements
(at peak divisional strength, 1944)
Panzer-Regiment 'Grossdeutschland'
Grenadier-Regiment 'Grossdeutschland'
Fusilier-Regiment 'Grossdeutschland'
Panzer-Artillerie-Regiment 'Grossdeutschland'
Panzeraufklärungs-Abteilung 'Grossdeutschland'
Heeres-Flak-Abteilung 'Grossdeutschland'
Sturmgeschützbrigade 'Grossdeutschland'
Panzer-Pionier-Bataillon 'Grossdeutschland'

A Gefreiter from Panzergrenadier-Regiment 'Grossdeutschland 2' with his wife and young children. Note the shoulder straps with the small numeral '2' just below the 'GD' cipher; this rare strap type was only worn for a short period in 1942–43.

Satellite units
Führer-Grenadier-Brigade
(expanded to divisional status early 1945)
Formed July 1944; first saw action in October 1944 around Gumbinnen and Goldap in East Prussia. Removed in November for rest and refit before being committed to the Ardennes offensive with 5. Panzerarmee. It provided rearguard cover for retreating units when the offensive collapsed, and was thereafter refitted as a Panzer-Division in February 1945. It was thrown into action at Stettin on the Oder in March 1945 and was involved in a failed attempt to recapture Küstrin. In the closing days of the war it was fighting around Vienna, and fought its way west to surrender to the Americans, but its personnel were promptly turned over to the Soviets. This unit also wore the *Grossdeutschland* cuffband. A special shoulder strap with the cipher 'FG' was produced but seems to have been worn only very rarely; it was in any case replaced by the standard 'GD' cipher in the autumn of 1944, and in early 1945 the unit ceased using a shoulder strap cipher.

The *Führerhauptquartier* cuffband, hand-embroidered in aluminium thread Sütterlin script on a black doeskin base. It was worn on the lower left sleeve by all troops during their attachment to Hitler's headquarters, e.g. the Führer-Begleit-Brigade drawn from 'GD' personnel.

Führer-Begleit-Brigade
(expanded to divisional status early 1945)
Initially a bodyguard unit for Hitler, it was expanded into an armoured brigade in November 1944. It too was used in the abortive Ardennes offensive before being thrown into defensive actions in East Prussia, after being expanded yet again to divisional status. Fighting around Vienna towards the end of the war, it was almost totally wiped out in

actions against the Red Army near Spremberg. Those members of the brigade actually on duty at Hitler's headquarters wore a cuffband in black with the legend *Führerhauptquartier* in silver; others used the standard *Grossdeutschland* cuffband. The standard 'GD' shoulder strap ciphers were used by this unit.

Panzergrenadier-Division 'Kurmark'
This late war creation, formed from GD replacement units in January 1945, was thrown into action on the Oder Front in February. In April it was involved in very heavy fighting around the Halbe Pocket, achieving impressive initial progress before being swamped when the front finally collapsed. Its remnants went into Soviet captivity.

'GD' divisional commanders
Oberstleutnant Wilhelm von Stockhausen (July 1939–February 1940)
Oberstleutnant Gerhard Graf von Schwerin (February–May 1940)
Oberst von Stockhausen (May 1940–August 1941)
Oberst Walter Hoernlein (August 1941–April 1942)
Generalmajor Walter Hoernlein (April 1942–April 1944)
Generalleutnant Hasso von Manteuffel (April–August 1944)
Oberst Karl Lorenz (September 1944–May 1945)

Special insignia
Cuffbands
The most significant piece of special insignia for most élite units was the cuffband. A cuffband was first authorised in June 1939, with the legend *Grossdeutschland* machine-woven in metallic aluminium thread Gothic script characters on a dark green rayon backing, with woven aluminium edge stripes. The cuffband was worn on the lower right sleeve, 15cm from the edge of the cuff. At some time in the summer of 1940 a new version was introduced with the inscription altered to read *Inf. Regt. Grossdeutschland*; so far no photographic evidence of its wear has emerged, but original surviving examples are known. These are of similar construction to the first pattern, being machine-woven in aluminium thread on a dark green rayon band.

The third, and most widely seen, version was introduced in 1939 and reverted to the single word *Grossdeutschland,* but this time hand-embroidered in aluminium bullion thread in old German Sütterlin script, and on a black rather than a dark green band. The base material was usually of a fine doeskin finish with edging in aluminium 'Russia' braid. This type has often been referred to as an 'officer's grade' band but it was in fact worn by all ranks. Although the first type was generally replaced by the Sütterlin script version by late 1940, photographic evidence clearly establishes that it continued to be worn by veterans of the original 'Grossdeutschland' regiment well into the war.

In around mid-1944 orders were issued standardising the manufacture of cuffbands in the interests of economy. The regulation issue *Grossdeutschland* bands produced after this time are machine-embroidered in silver-grey yarn on a black woollen badgecloth band with silver-grey Russia braid edging. Further, in November 1944 it was ordered that all cuffbands be made in a length of no more than 25cm so that the band would not reach all the way around the sleeve –

Leutnant Willi Heinrich from the Panzer-Abteilung of the Führer-Grenadier-Brigade. Although a special 'FG' cipher was created, it was used only for a very short time before being replaced with the standard 'GD' cipher as worn here.

ABOVE **This Feldwebel from the 'Grossdeutschland' Division is pictured during an attachment to the Wachregiment in Berlin. He retains his divisional cuffband but for the period of his attachment wears the Gothic 'W' cipher on his shoulder straps. (Chris Boonzaier)**

ABOVE RIGHT **Oberleutnant Karl Hausmann during his attachment to the Wachregiment. He wears the third-pattern Sütterlin script divisional cuffband, with gilt metal 'W' ciphers on his shoulder straps.**

a reasonable economy measure as the part to the inside of the sleeve would in any case remain unseen. Photographic evidence proves the use of these shortened bands, though their rarity suggests that sufficient stocks of full length bands must still have been available to meet normal needs.

A final version of the *Grossdeutschland* cuffband was introduced in 1944. This had the legend machine-embroidered in 'copperplate' handwriting-style script. Being introduced after the move to simple machine embroidery for cuffband manufacture, this type is almost invariably encountered in silver-grey yarn on black badgecloth, but a few original hand-embroidered aluminium thread examples have been noted – almost certainly privately commissioned.

Shoulder strap ciphers

In 1936 a special shoulder strap cipher consisting of the letter 'W' for Wache 'Guard', was introduced for wear by members of Wachregiment Berlin, the immediate forerunner of 'Grossdeutschland'. The cipher was machine-embroidered into the shoulder strap in white yarn for ranks up to Unteroffizier, stamped in white metal for senior NCOs (i.e. from Unteroffizier upwards) and in gilt metal for officers. Although officially replaced by the later 'GD' cipher, the 'W' cipher is known to have continued in use by personnel of the Wachbataillon element from 'Grossdeutschland' when on rotation duty in Berlin.

In June 1939, when the unit name was changed to 'Grossdeutschland', a special shoulder strap cipher was introduced consisting of the intertwined letters 'G' and 'D'. This was embroidered directly into the strap for ranks up to Unteroffizier, the colour of the embroidery matching the colour of the Waffenfarbe arm-of-service piping to the shoulder strap. For senior NCOs it was in white metal and for officers in gilt metal.

Before reorganisation into Grenadier and Fusilier Regiments, 'Grossdeutschland's armoured infantry regiments were numbered 1 and 2. Between March 1942 and June 1943 the appropriate numeral was worn on the shoulder strap below the 'GD' cipher, before being replaced with loops of coloured braid above and below the cipher in white or red respectively.

Other special insignia

The Flak-Abteilung 'Grossdeutschland' introduced, some time in 1943, a unique identifying sleeve badge consisting of a winged Flak shell,

woven in red yarn on an oval dark green base. It was worn on the upper right sleeve.

The Feldgendarmerietrupp 'Grossdeutschland' altered the standard military police gorget to produce their own unique unit version. A blackened metal plate emblazoned with the 'GD' cipher in white was added to the rear of the standard gorget plate, effectively filling in the gap in the half-moon shaped plate between the two suspension buttons.

Special uniforms

'Grossdeutschland' was unique in being the only élite unit to have its own special pattern of uniform. This was designed and launched in 1939, but was never generally issued, though it is believed it was intended to be the standard dress uniform for the unit after the anticipated final victory. The uniform consisted of a special Waffenrock-style tunic and greatcoat, the headgear and trousers being standard issue.

(Left) The special shoulder strap for those serving with the guard detachment in Berlin; in this case the rank is Feldwebel. The 'W' was embroidered for enlisted ranks, in white metal for senior NCOs and gilt metal for officers. (Centre) A rare shoulder strap from Panzergrenadier-Regiment 'Grossdeutschland 2', for the rank of Unterfeldwebel. (Right) Piping and embroidered cipher in orange on a field-grey strap for a member of the 'GD' divisional Feldgendarmerie troop.

The tunic was in pale grey green with dark green collar and cuff facings. The collar *Litzen* were of a special pattern, being much longer and narrower than the norm and without Waffenfarbe underlay; a single bar was worn by NCOs and a double bar by other ranks – the narrower NCO model allowing space for NCO *Tresse* braid along the top and front edges of the collar. The extreme edge of the collar was piped in white infantry Waffenfarbe colour. The 'French' cuffs also differed from the standard Waffenrock. As well as a normal turn-back cuff in dark green they had dark green vertical patches with a straight forward edge and scalloped rear edge. These dark green facings were also piped in white. Each of the vertical cuff patches bore three single strips of braid *Litzen* each with an aluminium button. This tunic was worn with the first type machine-woven aluminium-on-green Gothic script cuffband, and with the 'GD' shoulder strap ciphers. There were no pockets; the tunic was fastened by eight silvered aluminium buttons, and the front edge was also piped in white.

A special greatcoat was also designed to be worn with this uniform, differing from the standard issue in having white piping around the dark green collar collar and the turnback cuffs.

'FELDHERRNHALLE'

'Feldherrnhalle' was similar in some ways to 'Grossdeutschland' in being a unit whose recruitment, unlike that of most army units, was not restricted to a specific region or city but covered all corners of the Reich. 'Feldherrnhalle' was different, however, in that its traditional links were not with the German Army as such but with the SA, and specifically with the SA Regiment (Standarte) of the same name, with which it maintained close links. A large proportion of 'Feldherrnhalle's' manpower were SA members; this political aspect, however, does not detract from the fact that the Army unit was a high quality formation which earned its categorisation as an élite.

The 'Feldherrnhalle' Division's origins can be traced back to two separate earlier formations, 93. Infanterie-Division and 60. Infanterie-Division. The first of these was formed from reservists in Berlin in September 1939, its major components being Infanterie-Regiment 270, IR 271 and IR 272. Too late to take part in the Polish campaign, it was based in the Saar area in 1940 and took part in the attack on the Maginot Line near Saarbrucken in the summer of that year. After spending some time on garrison duty in France, 93. Infanterie-Division moved to Poland in preparation for the launching of Operation 'Barbarossa'.

As part of Heeresgruppe Nord, the 93rd Division advanced into the northern part of the Soviet Union during the drive towards Leningrad. It took heavy losses, around two-thirds of its strength being killed or wounded by October 1941. Remaining in the northern sector of the front, in the autumn of 1942 Infanterie-Regiment 271 was given the honour title Infanterie-Regiment 'Feldherrnhalle' in recognition of its link with the SA. In the spring of 1943 the division was withdrawn into Poland for rest and refitting, and IR 271 was moved to France where it was used to form the nucleus of 60. Panzergrenadier-Division. The 93rd Infantry Division subsequently moved back to the Eastern Front in the area around Leningrad, where it eventually received Infanterie-Regiment 273 as replacement for IR 271. It fought in the withdrawal from Leningrad and defensive actions in the Kurland pocket, whence it was evacuated by sea into East Prussia. It was destroyed in combat with the Red Army in March 1945.

The 60. Infanterie-Division was formed in 1939 in Danzig, drawing heavily on personnel from the Heimwehr Danzig (an SS home guard unit) and the SA Brigade Ehrhardt. It took part in the actions at the Westerplatte in September 1939, where the shots that opened World War II were fired. It served in France in 1940, and took part in the invasion of Yugoslavia in 1941. During Operation 'Barbarossa' the division saw action in many of the great battles in the Ukraine, the Donetz Basin, at Kiev, Rostov and Kharkov. Involved in the push to the River Volga in 1942, it was one of the divisions caught up and destroyed in the Stalingrad Cauldron in early 1943.

In the summer of 1943 the 60th Division was re-formed in France, this time as a Panzergrenadier formation, based around Infanterie-Regiment 271 'Feldherrnhalle'. Initially based in southern France, it moved to the Eastern Front in the autumn of 1943 and distinguished itself in combat at the battles of Vitebsk and Narva. It formed part of Heeresgruppe Mitte during the defensive battles following the launch of the great Soviet summer offensive of 1944. The division was smashed during the fiercely fought battles along the River Dnieper and its commander, Generalmajor

The traditional roots of 'Feldherrnhalle' were entirely political. This SA-Brigadeführer reporting to Reichsmarschall Göring wears the same gorget and cuffband as adopted by the Army's 'Feldherrnhalle' units – see Plate B. (Josef Charita)

Steinkeller, was captured. It retreated into Hungary, where its remnants were surrounded and destroyed in the battle for Budapest.

In 1944 a decision was taken in principle to form a 'Feldherrnhalle Armoured Corps' along the same lines as Panzer-Korps 'Grossdeutschland'. Also formed around this time were Panzer-Brigade 106 'Feldherrnhalle' and Panzer-Brigade 110 'Feldherrnhalle'. The latter was eventually absorbed into 13. Panzer-Division, which in turn was redesignated as Panzer-Division 'Feldherrnhalle'. While Panzer-Brigade 106 'Feldherrnhalle' fought in the West, Panzer-Division 'Feldherrnhalle' (formerly 13. Panzer-Division) was redesignated Panzer-Division 'Feldherrnhalle 2'. This was the formation which, with Panzergrenadier-Division 'Feldherrnhalle' (formerly 60. Panzergrenadier-Division, and subsequently redesignated Panzer-Division 'Feldherrnhalle 1'), would form Panzer-Korps 'Feldherrnhalle'. The newly formed corps spent the remaining months of the war fighting on the borders between Hungary, Czechoslovakia and Austria.

Major elements (1943)
Panzergrenadier-Regiment 'Feldherrnhalle'
Fusilier-Regiment 'Feldherrnhalle'
Panzer-Abteilung 'Feldherrnhalle'
Artillerie-Regiment 'Feldherrnhalle'
Panzeraufklärungs-Abteilung 'Feldherrnhalle'
Pionier-Bataillon 'Feldherrnhalle'

Divisional commanders
Generalleutnant Otto Kohlermann (June 1943–April 1944)
Generalmajor Friedrich Karl Steinkeller (April–July 1944)
Generalleutnant Günther Pape (July 1944–May 1945)

Special insignia
Cuffbands
The Army 'Feldherrnhalle' units inherited the cuffband worn by the élite SA-Standarte 'Feldherrnhalle', woven in brown rayon with metallic silver edging and the title *Feldherrnhalle* in Sütterlin script. This lettering might be machine-embroidered in silver-grey yarn, machine-woven in flat aluminium thread, or hand-embroidered in aluminium thread. The cuffband was worn on the lower left sleeve, 15cm from the cuff.

In 1943 a fully machine-woven version of the cuffband was produced in so-called BeVo style, in pale grey artificial silk on brown. This pattern was worn only by the Army 'Feldherrnhalle' units, not the SA. Examples have also been noted machine-embroidered in silver-grey yarn on brown woollen badgecloth and without edge stripes; these are believed to be late war Army patterns.

Under magnification the Unteroffizier at right can be seen to wear the *Feldherrnhalle* cuffband and the SA-Kampfrune insignia on his shoulder straps. Full issue of the special unit insignia seems to have been unusual in this formation; many photographed personnel lack either the shoulder strap insignia (usually), the cuffband, or both. Presumably large stocks of cuffbands were made pre-war for the SA unit, so these would have been relatively easily sourced. (Robert Noss)

Shoulder strap ciphers

The Army 'Feldherrnhalle' units were permitted to wear the *'Kampfrune'* emblem worn on the straps by the SA-Standarte 'Feldherrnhalle'. This comprised three horizontal *'Wolfsangel'* runes superimposed on a single vertical rune; in the centre was a small disc with the 'SA' runic emblem.

The cipher was machine-embroidered directly into the shoulder strap for ranks up to Unteroffizier, stamped in white metal for senior NCOs and in bronze or gilt metal for officers.

A shoulder strap for the rank of Unterfeldwebel, in field-grey cloth typical of mid-war manufacture, with the SA-Kampfrune in white metal, above two examples of the *Feldherrnhalle* cuffband showing the differing shades of brown base material which may be encountered. The lettering on these examples is machine-woven, but embroidered lettering was also used.

Oberst Alfons König, commander of Infanterie-Regiment 'List'. He wears the unit cuffband on the lower left sleeve. (Josef Charita)

Gorgets

Standard bearers in the Army 'Feldherrnhalle' units wore the same special pattern of gorget as did the SA-Standarte, rather than the Army's equivalent. The SA piece comprised a plain half-moon shaped gorget with a large national emblem in the centre; there was no other embellishment to the plate other than this eagle and swastika, so the gorget was much plainer-looking than its elaborate Army counterpart. It was coloured matt silver with a bronzed national emblem, and was suspended around the neck on a plain open-link chain.

Unit colours

'Feldherrnhalle' was also unique amongst Army units in that its colours were not of the normal Army regimental pattern. Instead 'Feldherrnhalle' adopted the 'Deutschland Erwache' type of vexillum standard used by political organisations – specifically, the same as carried by the SA-Standarte 'Feldherrnhalle'. This featured a large metal eagle and swastika finial over a rectangular plaque bearing the legend *Feldherrnhalle* (in place of a regional title). From this was suspended a square red banner with white disk and black swastika, the edges fringed in black and white.

INFANTERIE-REGIMENTER 119 & 19 'LIST'

In 1935, Infanterie-Regiment 19 was selected to carry the traditions of the 16th Royal Bavarian Reserve Regiment 'List', the unit with which Adolf Hitler had served during the Great War. This lasted until 1939 when the lineage was passed to Infanterie-Regiment 119, part of 57. Infanterie-Division.

This division acquitted itself exceptionally well in combat during both the Polish campaign and the fighting in the West. It was responsible for blunting a strong French counter-attack at Abbeville led by Gen. Charles de Gaulle; it inflicted heavy losses on the French after initially suffering severe casualties itself – its light 3.7cm anti-tank guns proved all but useless against the heavily armoured French tanks. The arrival of an 8.8cm Flak unit turned the tables, however, and in two days of fierce fighting over 100 French tanks were destroyed and De Gaulle's counter-attack was halted.

For the invasion of the Soviet Union in June 1941, 57. Infanterie-Division served with XLVIII Panzerkorps in the dash across southern Russia, incurring heavy losses along the way. It fought at Kursk in July 1943 as part of Generaloberst Hoth's 4. Panzerarmee. In February 1944 the division was caught in the Cherkassy Pocket and only broke out at the cost of many casualties. After a brief period of rest and recuperation the division rejoined the fray with Heeresgruppe Mitte in the central sector of the Eastern Front. It was surrounded at Minsk with XXVII Armeekorps, and the bulk of the division was destroyed. Shortly thereafter the surviving remnants were disbanded.

Divisional commanders, 57. Infanterie-Division

Generalleutnant Oskar Blümm (September 1939–September 1941)

General Anton Dostler (September 1941–April 1942)

Generalleutnant Oskar Blümm (April–October 1942)

General Friedrich Siebert (October 1942–February 1943)

Generalleutnant Otto von Fretter-Pico (February–September 1943)

Generalleutnant Vincenz Müller (September 1943)

Generalmajor Adolf Trowitz (September 1943–July 1944)

This Leutnant in attendance upon GFM von Rundstedt does not appear to have the Kampfrune insignia on his shoulder strap, but does wear a fine example of the *Feldherrnhalle* divisional cuffband.

On the destruction of Infanterie-Regiment 119 with the 57. Infanterie-Division, the traditions of the Regiment 'List' reverted to Infanterie-Regiment 19, part of 7. Infanterie-Division. This division had served as part of Heeresgruppe Mitte with XLVI Panzerkorps and had barely escaped destruction in the great Soviet summer offensive of 1944. It carried out a fighting retreat through Poland until finally cut off by the last great Soviet offensive of the war at the Hela Peninsula at the mouth of the River Vistula, where it surrendered on 8 May 1945.

The *Infanterie-Regiment List* cuffband. This was machine-embroidered in silver-grey cotton thread on a dark green base for all ranks; no hand-embroidered wire officer's versions are known.

Divisional commanders, 7. Infanterie-Division, 1944–45

Generalmajor Hans Traut (December 1943–February 1944)

Generalleutnant Fritz-George von Rappard (February–August 1944)

Generalmajor Alois Weber (August 1944)

Generalleutnant Fritz-George von Rappard (August 1944–February 1945)

Generalmajor Rudolf Noak (February–May 1945)

Special insignia

Cuffband

The only special emblem worn by the regiment was its distinctive cuffband, authorised on

Soldiers from Infanterie-Regiment 'List' crossing an anti-tank ditch during the advance through Soviet Russia; none appear to wear the cuffband on their combat uniforms. Note, however, that the company bugler at left does carry his instrument in the field. (Robert Noss)

12 November 1943; the first recipient was the regimental commander Oberst Alfons König. It was made in dark green doeskin wool, with silver-grey Russia braid edging, and with the legend *Infanterie-Regiment List* machine-embroidered in silver-grey thread in 'copperplate'-style handwriting script. The band was worn on the lower left sleeve 15cm from the cuff.

PANZERGRENADIER-DIVISION 'BRANDENBURG'

This formation owed its origins to the élite 'Brandenburg' commando unit established in October 1939 under the innocent-sounding title of Bau-Lehr-Kompanie 800 ('800th Construction Demonstration Company'). This special operations unit of trained saboteurs came under the direct control of the Abwehr, the German Military Intelligence service. In January 1940 it was reorganised as Bau-Lehr-Bataillon zbV 800 ('800th Special Purpose Construction Demonstration Battalion'), and played a significant part in the campaign in the West. One well-known operation in which the battalion were involved was the capture of the bridges over the Juliana Canal in the Netherlands, carried out by 'Brandenburgers' dressed as Dutch soldiers. It has been estimated that fully 75 per cent of the unit's personnel received the Iron Cross for actions during the Westfeldzug. A huge range of skills and foreign language abilities was represented within the battalion; and English-speaking Brandenburgers were intended to be used, in British uniform, as an advance guard to the invasion force had the intended Operation 'Sealion' gone ahead.

The Brandenburgers fought in virtually every campaign on every front. Following the invasion of the Soviet Union in June 1941, unit personnel dressed in Soviet uniforms infiltrated columns of enemy wounded being moved back from the front, enabling them to move behind enemy lines and seize the vital Dvina River bridge. The regiment rarely operated as a single entity, its specialist nature dictating that elements be detached for dispersed special operations over several fronts. In 1942 the parent unit was raised to divisional status, its new complement including

The sleeve patch for Jäger units; this example is machine-embroidered, but woven versions were also produced. Below it is shown the *Brandenburg* cuffband; this was manufactured in one style only, machine-embroidered in silver-grey cotton yarn on a black wool base.

a coastal raider detachment with volunteers from the Navy, and a battalion of renegade Russian volunteers.

Detachments operated in the Balkans in late 1943, being heavily involved in anti-partisan actions in Greece and Yugoslavia and playing a significant part in the capture of the islands of Cos and Leros from the British. Elements of the division took part in the occupation of Budapest in March 1944; and were actively involved in Operation 'Rösselsprung', the attempt to capture Tito at his Drvar headquarters.

During the investigations into the 20 July 1944 attempt to assassinate Hitler several Brandenburgers were implicated. His trust in these commandos gone, Hitler transferred responsibility for such special operations as had traditionally fallen to the Brandenburgers to SS commando units under SS-Obersturmbannführer Otto Skorzeny. In October 1944, 'Brandenburg' was redesignated as a conventional Panzergrenadier-Division, and was finally ready for action in its new role in December 1944. Thrown into battle on the rapidly crumbling Eastern Front, it was steadily worn down in strength, ending the war in Moravia. Many of its survivors were captured by the Red Army or murdered by revenge-hungry Czechs; but some, using their old special operations skills, managed to escape to the West posing as refugees.

Major elements (as division, 1944–45)
Panzer-Regiment 'Brandenburg'
Jäger-Regiment 1 'Brandenburg'
Jäger-Regiment 2 'Brandenburg'
Panzerjäger-Bataillon 'Brandenburg'
Artillerie-Regiment 'Brandenburg'
Heeres-Flak-Abteilung 'Brandenburg'
Aufklärungs-Abteilung 'Brandenburg'
Pionier-Bataillon 'Brandenburg'

Unit commanders
Oberst Haehling von Lanzenhauer (1940–43)
Generalmajor von Pfuhlstein (1943–44)
Generalleutnant Kühlwein (September–October 1944)
Generalmajor Hermann Schulte Heuthaus (October 1944–May 1945)

Special insignia
The Brandenburg division was authorised its own cuffband on 17 August 1944; personnel had been permitted to wear the *Grossdeutschland* cuffband. The new cuffband was made from black badgecloth or doeskin finish wool, with *Brandenburg* machine-embroidered in silver-grey thread in Gothic script. Being introduced only in 1944, the official issue pattern was not produced in hand-embroidered bullion thread, only in silver grey cotton yarn.

Brandenburg units were also authorised to wear the special sleeve patch for Jäger troops, consisting

Oberstleutnant Karl-Heinz Oesterwirtz of Bau-Lehr-Regiment zbV 800 at the time of the award of the Oakleaves to his Knight's Cross. The rare *Brandenburg* cuffband can be seen on the lieutenant-colonel's lower right sleeve, and above it the embroidered oakleaf sleeve badge for Jäger units.

A member of a Brandenburg commando unit involved in the capture of the island of Cos in early 1944. He wears Army lightweight tropical field dress, with the peaked field cap thrust into the front of his tunic. Note, however, the rare Army parachutist's badge on his left breast pocket. By this stage in the war Brandenburgers were the only servicemen being awarded this Army paratroop qualification badge. (Mike Bischoff)

of a spray of three pale green oakleaves within a pale grey rope-effect border, all on a dark green, or later field-grey patch. This was worn on the upper right sleeve.

KAVALLERIE-REGIMENT 5 'FELDMARSCHALL VON MACKENSEN'

Despite the image of the German Army portrayed in most wartime newsreels as being heavily mechanised, the Wehrmacht fielded a sizeable number of mounted troops – particularly on the Eastern Front, where horsed cavalry played an important part in the reconnaissance role and also in the war against the partisans.[1] Although the 1st Cavalry Division was withdrawn at the end of 1941, and mounted troops were only found within reconnaissance units for the next 18 months, in June 1943 both Heeresgruppe Nord and Heeresgruppe Süd were allocated their own cavalry regiments, entitled respectively Kavallerie-Regiment Nord and Kavallerie-Regiment Süd, under the command of Oberstleutnant Carl Prinz zu Salm. In May 1944 the regiments were renamed as Kavallerie-Regimenter 42 and 41 respectively, and administratively merged to form 42. Kavallerie-Brigade. Its principal elements were Kavallerie-Regimenter 2 and 41; schwere Kavallerie-Bataillon 4 (mot); Artillerie-Abteilung Süd, as well as heavy mortar and signals detachments.

A few days later, however, the former Kavallerie-Regiment Nord was renamed Kavallerie-Regiment 5, in reference to the old 5th Cavalry Regiment of the Imperial German Army; henceforth the unit would carry the traditions of that esteemed regiment. The 4th Cavalry Brigade was expanded to divisional status in February 1945; it operated in Hungary for two months before withdrawing into Austria where it fought out the remainder of the war in actions against the Red Army, before finally surrendering to the British.

Known commanders, 4. Kavallerie-Division
Generalleutnant Rudolf Hoste (February–March 1945)
Generalleutnant Helmuth von Grolman (March–May 1945)

Special insignia
Cuffband
A cuffband was introduced for Kavallerie-Regiment 5 on 6 December 1944, the occasion of Field Marshal von Mackensen's 95th birthday. An example of it was presented to him at Erbhof Brüssow in Pomerania in a special ceremony attended by Generalfeldmarschall Keitel from the Oberkommando der Wehrmacht, and also by an officer, an NCO and a Gefreiter from the regiment. It had been doubted that cuffbands apart from this special presentation piece were ever issued; but rare wartime photographs show several members of the unit, including the regimental

1 See MAA 361, *Axis Cavalry in World War II*

An unidentified Knight's Cross winner with the death's-head tradition badge as worn by Kavallerie-Regiment 5 in his cap. The design of the death's-head varied; this one seems to be the standard pattern as used on Panzer collar patches.

commander Oberstleutnant Sauer and Majors Bullingen and Bischoff-Sonsfeld, wearing it on the lower right sleeve. It must be said, however, that many other personnel shown in the same photos are not wearing the band, so it is still thought likely that only very limited numbers were made.

The band was 3.2cm wide, made from black wool with silver-grey Russia braid edging and the legend *Feldmarschall v. Mackensen* machine-embroidered in silver-grey Latin script. A number of examples have appeared post-war, presumably made as commemorative pieces for veterans; some are quite crude and others extremely elaborate, including one exceptionally high quality piece which has the military rank expressed in full as *Generalfeldmarschall von Mackensen* in Sütterlin script. The standard Latin script version is the only type for which evidence of actual wartime use exists.

It has been reported that due to the difficulty in obtaining supplies of regulation issue cuffbands, local 'cottage industry' facilities were used – specifically, that nuns at a local convent were paid to use their embroidery skills to make up examples of the band. This suggestion is perfectly logical and closely parallels the circumstances of manufacture of the *Kurland* campaign cuffband.[2]

An example of the new *Feldmarschall v. Mackensen* cuffband was presented to the field-marshal on the occasion of his 95th birthday on 6 December 1944 by General-feldmarschall Keitel, attended by an officer, an NCO and an enlisted man of Kavallerie-Regiment 5. (Josef Charita)

RIGHT The *Feldmarschall v. Mackensen* cuffband was officially produced in only one version, machine-embroidered in silver–grey cotton thread on a black wool base. Some privately commissioned wire-embroidered examples of 'officer quality' are known.

Shoulder strap and cap emblem

Kavallerie-Regiment 5 were authorised to wear on the shoulder straps a death's-head tradition badge; this was the 'jawless' or 'Prussian' type, identical to that worn on the collar patch by Panzer troops. It was embroidered in cavalry golden-yellow thread directly into the shoulder strap for ranks up to Unteroffizier, and stamped in gilt metal for senior NCOs and officers. The same tradition badge was also worn on both peaked service caps and field caps, between the eagle and swastika national emblem and the cockade in national colours.

Arm patch

An unusual arm patch was worn on the upper right sleeve by some members of 4. Kavallerie-Division – including Kavallerie-Regiment 5 – in the last weeks of the war. This was an entirely unofficial insignia, and judging by the relative crudity of surviving examples it seems to have been made up by local 'cottage industry' facilities rather than being commissioned from a trade manufacturer. It consists of a yellow woollen shield with a black border, upon which two opposed horses' heads are worked in black.[3]

2 See MAA 365, *World War II German Battle Insignia*
3 See MAA 365, *World War II German Battle Insignia*, Plate H

44. REICHSGRENADIER-DIVISION 'HOCH UND DEUTSCHMEISTER'

The German Army's original 44. Infanterie-Division was raised in Vienna, based on the former Austrian Army's Viennese 4th Infantry Regiment, which bore the tradition title 'Hoch und Deutschmeister'. The division fought well in Poland in 1939, making such rapid progress as part of Heeresgruppe Süd that it found itself well within the area allocated to the Soviet Union – it has been estimated that the division's average rate of advance was as much as 20 miles per day. During the Westfeldzug the division followed in the wake of Panzergruppe Kleist, taking part in the attack over the Somme and into the Weygand Line, resulting in heavy casualties against a determined French resistance. The division's first Knight's Cross was won by Oberstleutnant Karl Eibl for his part in the capture of Chuignolles. Elements of the 44th Division were also responsible for capturing Beaugency on the Loire without loss on 18 June, winning another Knight's Cross, this time for Leutnant Karl-Heinz Noak. Following the French surrender the division spent ten months on occupation duties around La Rochelle before moving to occupied Poland in March 1941 for a period of intensive training.

In Operation 'Barbarossa' in June 1941 the 44th served as part of 1. Panzergruppe on the southern sector of the front, and took fairly heavy casualties breaking through a series of Soviet bunker complexes. As the tanks rapidly pushed forward it was left to 44. Infanterie-Division to defend the flank of the Panzergruppe against attacks by Soviet stragglers and partisans coming out of the Pripet Marshes to the north. In August the division took part in the attack on Kiev, crossing the Dnieper near Gornostaipol. Once again, the tanks carried out a classic pincer movement to encircle Kiev before moving on, and the division was left to deal with the Soviet forces trapped in Kiev city. Slowed down at first by the onset of the autumn mud (the 'Schlammzeit'), and later by the coming of winter, 44. Infanterie-Division ended its first year in Russia in defensive positions on the Donetz, which it held resolutely in the face of strong enemy counter-attacks.

In 1942 the 44th Division formed part of the 6. Armee drive towards the Volga with the goal of capturing Stalingrad. The division provided cover to the northern flank along the River Don to the north-west of Stalingrad, and saw very heavy fighting before slowly being forced eastwards into the pocket as the German forces were gradually surrounded. It suffered the same fate as the rest of Von Paulus' army, being destroyed in Stalingrad in February 1943.

Major Arnulf Abele, commander of I Bataillon, Reichsgrenadier-Regiment 'Hoch und Deutsch-meister'. Under magnification the 'Stalingrad Cross' shoulder strap emblem can just be seen at the far right of this image. For service in Italy he wears a high quality privately tailored tropical uniform.

Shortly afterwards a new 44. Division was raised in Austria under the honour title Reichsgrenadier-Division 'Hoch und Deutschmeister'. It served briefly in Northern Italy as part of Heeresgruppe B under Rommel. At first its Austrian troops enjoyed good relations with the local populace until, after Italy's unilateral surrender, it was obliged to take part in the disarming of Italian Army units in the area. It subsequently carried out operations against Italian, Croatian and Slovenian partisans between Gärz and Fiume, before being inserted into the front line south of Rome. Here it served for over a year in constant combat, its reputation for reliability increasing with each battle it fought. In 1943/44 the division was involved in the defensive battles along the Sangro and Rapido Rivers and in all three of the Cassino battles, before withdrawing across the Abruzzi Mountains.

After holding defensive positions on the Tiber and in the Apenine Mountains it spent a very brief period in rest and recuperation in early November 1944, but was soon despatched to Hungary. Until March 1945 the division fought against the advancing Red Army before withdrawing gradually from Hungary into eastern Germany. It was able to retreat westwards and avoided Soviet captivity, surrendering to US troops at Hohenfurth on 10 May 1945.

Main elements
Grenadier-Regiment 131
Grenadier-Regiment 132
Grenadier-Regiment 134
Panzerjäger-Abteilung 46
Aufklärungs-Abteilung 44
Artillerie-Regiment 96
Nachrichten-Abteilung 64
Pionier-Bataillon 80

Divisional commanders
Generalleutnant Albrecht Schubert (September–October 1939)
General Friedrich Siebert (October 1939–May 1942)
Generalleutnant Heinrich Deboi (May 1942–January 1943)
Generalleutnant Dr Franz Bayer (March 1943–January 1944)
Generalleutnant Dr Fritz Franek (January–May 1944)
Generalleutnant Bruno Ortner (May–June 1944)
Generalleutnant Hans-Günther von Rost (June 1944–March 1945)
Oberst Hoffmann (March–May 1945)

Special insignia
Cuffband
A cuffband was certainly authorised on 26 February 1945, and a number of examples are known which appear to relate to this formation. All bear the legend *Hoch und Deutschmeister*, machine-embroidered in silver-grey yarn; some are in Latin script and others in Gothic. While these have generally been regarded as of post-war origin, in recent years there has been some suggestion that the different styles of embroidery may have had some significance: Gothic script on dark green for the divisional logistics element, Gothic script on black for Grenadier-Regiment 134 'Hoch und Deutschmeister', and Latin script on black for other sub-units.

The famous 'Stalingrad Cross' shoulder strap emblem in yellow metal, with the arms of the cross infilled with light blue paint. Below it are the three alleged variants of the unit cuffband: (top) Gothic script on green for the logistics element, (centre) Latin script on black for other divisional units, (bottom) Gothic script on black for Grenadier-Regiment 134. There is no known evidence that these were ever issued and worn.

It is not impossible that some may have been manufactured in the last weeks of the war but never issued. Until positive proof emerges these pieces must be considered suspect; but collectors should always remember that for many years the *Metz 1944* cuffband was believed never to have been manufactured during the war, but is now firmly established from wartime photographs to have been made, issued and worn, albeit in small numbers.

Shoulder strap emblem

A special insignia, widely referred to as the 'Stalingrad Cross', was worn on the shoulder strap by members of the divisional staff and of Infanterie-Regiment 134 'Hoch und Deutschmeister'. This was stamped from sheet metal and featured a cross of the type worn by the Order of Teutonic Knights, with a shield in the centre bearing the German national emblem over a scroll with the legend 'Stalingrad'. The field of each arm of the cross was painted in blue (see Plate C4). No embroidered version has yet been noted, so it may well be that the metal cross was intended for wear by all ranks. Original examples of this insignia are rare and it has been widely faked.

116. PANZER-DIVISION ('WINDHUND')

This formation, unofficially nicknamed the 'Greyhound Division', was created only in March 1944, by a merger of the remnants of the battered 16. Panzergrenadier-Division – which donated Panzer-Abteilung 116, later re-formed as Panzer-Regiment 16 – and 179. (Reserve) Panzer-Division. Since it was formed from existing units only limited time was necessary for training and working up. Within three months most of the division was in position on the banks of the Seine awaiting the anticipated Allied invasion. However, the Panzer-Regiment's I Abteilung was still at the Gräfenwohr tank training grounds re-equipping with new Panthers; and its II Abteilung in France still had a number of older PzKw IVs and even a few obsolete PzKw IIIs.

In the event the division was not committed to action until July, attached to XLVII Panzerkorps as part of 7. Armee in Rommel's Heeresgruppe B. It participated in the German counter-attack at Mortain, one of the biggest tank battles in the West, which failed to halt the US armoured break-out (Operation 'Cobra'); the 116th was gradually pushed back into the Falaise Pocket, from which it only escaped after suffering very heavy losses. After its withdrawal from Normandy the division's strength was down to a mere 600 men and just 12 tanks; but it was soon tasked with defending the border city of Aachen. The rump of the division succeeded in fending off the first US attacks against the Westwall before finally being driven back. Withdrawn to Dusseldorf for a brief period of refitting and rebuilding, 116. Panzer-Division returned to the Aachen area in early October 1944, but still at only around 50 per cent of its original strength, and with only 40 tanks. On 21 October, Aachen became the first German city to fall to the Americans.

In late October, 116. Panzer-Division was committed to the defensive battles against US forces in the Hürtgen Forest. On 8 November it achieved a significant victory (almost any victory seemed significant at this stage of the war) when it retook the town of Schmidt from the US 28th Infantry Division during fierce fighting in which it lost just 15 tanks.

Following this success the division was moved back from the front line to prepare for its part in the forthcoming Ardennes offensive, Operation 'Wacht am Rhein'. It was one of the spearhead formations on the southern flank of the offensive, where it fought with distinction. On the failure of the operation it was moved to Kleve on the Dutch border, facing a mixture of troops from the US 9th Army advancing from the south, and Canadian 1st Army and British XXX Corps troops in the north. The 116th found itself in danger of being trapped in the Wessel Pocket, and on 5 March 1945 was forced to withdraw over the Rhine, destroying the bridge behind it.

The division then became part of XLVII Panzerkorps in Armeegruppe H, and was tasked with halting the advance of US forces to the south of the River Lippe on 24 March. Over the next two days the by now once again seriously weakened 'Greyhound' Division halted all attempts by US troops to advance eastwards, but was eventually forced to withdraw when the British 6th Guards Armoured Brigade successfully outflanked it. April 1945 found the remnants of the division defending the north flank of the Ruhr Valley where, on 18 April, its survivors surrendered to the US 9th Army when resistance in the Ruhr Pocket finally collapsed.

Like the Panzer-Lehr-Division, 116. Panzer had shown that when new formations were created around a strong nucleus of experienced veterans and equipped to a high standard, a very high level of performance and reliability could be expected. These qualities were of little use, however, when faced with lack of fuel, supplies and replacements, and with overwhelming enemy superiority, especially in the air.

Major Heinz-Gunther Guderian, son of Generaloberst Heinz Guderian, senior staff officer (Ia) of 116. Panzer-Division. Below him is shown an example of the divisional emblem worn as a badge on the left side of the peaked cap and field cap.

Main elements

Panzer-Regiment 16
Panzergrenadier-Regiment 60
Panzergrenadier-Regiment 156
Panzer-Artillerie-Regiment 146
Panzeraufklärungs-Abteilung 116
Heeres-Flak-Abteilung 281
Panzerjäger-Abteilung 226
Panzerpionier-Bataillon 675

Divisional commanders

Generalmajor Gerard Müller (March–May 1944)
General Gerhard Graf von Schwerin (May–September 1944)
Generalmajor Heinrich Voigtsberger (September 1944)
Generalmajor Siegfried von Waldeburg (September 1944–May 1945)

Special insignia

Only one special insignia was worn by this unit, in the form of an unofficial cap badge. This consisted of a small horizontal oval zinc plate with two prongs on the reverse for fitting to the cap. It was painted black with a raised silver rim, enclosing a raised silver greyhound (the *Windhund*) at full stretch, above a stylised ground line with three clumps of grass.

It was worn on the left side of the field cap and on the left side of the band of the peaked service cap. This insignia has been widely faked in the post-war years.

21. PANZER-DIVISION

This division was originally formed as **5. Leichte Division** in late 1940, incorporating Panzer-Regiment 5 which was transferred from 3. Panzer-Division – a Berlin unit first raised in 1935. The manpower of the 5th Light Division retained the predominantly Prussian/Silesian mix of 3. Panzer-Division. It was sent to North Africa in spring 1941, and shortly after its arrival took an active part in the Afrikakorps' first drive towards Egypt and the attack on Tobruk. In the summer of 1941 it was enlarged by the arrival of Panzergrenadier-Regiment 104, and redesignated as 21. Panzer-Division.

The division became one of the premier formations of Rommel's Panzerarmee Afrika, heavily engaged in all the major battles of the campaign. During the British Operation 'Crusader' in November 1941 it inflicted serious losses on the attacking 7th Armoured Brigade, but fought itself virtually into the ground in the process, ending the battle with no tanks remaining. It retreated into Cyrenaica and then, re-equipped, took part in the May 1942 counter-offensive, retaking Benghazi before going on to overrun the Gazala Line. It took part in the attack on Tobruk, but during the first failed attempt to capture the port the divisional commander was blamed by Rommel for his lack of success and removed from his post. The division continued to play a major part in Rommel's attempts on the El Alamein line that summer. At Second Alamein in October it was ground down to a remnant of its former strength, counting just 12 remaining tanks in November when the full-scale Axis retreat began.

The division withdrew in good order and with excellent discipline, providing a rearguard for the German retreat. It was reinforced in Tunisia in February 1943 and most of its losses in tanks were made good. It then took part in the battles around Sidi Bou Zid and Sbeitla, and at Kasserine Pass it inflicted serious losses on the recently arrived American II Corps. Worn down by attrition and lack of fuel and supplies, 21st Panzer was finally trapped in northern Tunisia with the rest of Panzerarmee Afrika, its remnants surrendering on 13 May 1943.

Shortly thereafter the division was re-formed in Normandy; a considerable cadre of former 'Africans' who had served with the original 21st ensured continuity of the division's traditions and ésprit de corps. The new formation was principally built around the former Panzer-Regiment 100 (subsequently renumbered as

Leutnant Johannes Lutz, commander of the Divisions-Begleit-Kompanie of 116. Panzer-Division. The field-grey version of the special uniform for armoured personnel was widely worn in this division, even by non-armoured units.

Panzer-Regiment 22), but this unit was initially equipped with obsolete French tanks of dubious combat value. By the summer of 1944 German tanks had replaced many of these, but even then there was a fair representation of obsolete vehicles such as the PzKw IVB and IVC and even a few old PzKw IIIs. The newly formed division remained on occupation duty in France, being declared unfit for service on the Eastern Front due to its poor equipment.

In June 1944, 21. Panzer-Division was the only armoured unit to actually counter-attack the Allied landings on D-Day. Elements of the Panzer-Regiment were on exercises when the invasion was reported, but being armed only with training ammunition they had to be hurriedly recalled to be issued with live rounds. In the weeks which followed the division took a hammering as it doggedly defended its area in front of Caen, contributing significantly to the severe delay imposed on the Allied timetable. After escaping from the Allied pincer attack around the Falaise Pocket the division was used as a mobile 'fire brigade' on the south-west sector of the Western Front. The Panzer-Regiment's commander, Oberst Hermann von Oppeln-Bronikowski, was decorated with the Oakleaves to his Knight's Cross in recognition of his regiment's performance in Normandy. In January 1945, 21. Panzer took part in the German push towards Strasbourg, before being transferred to the southern sector of the Russian Front, where it ended the war.

Major Hermann von Oppeln-Bronikowski, commander of the tank regiment in 21. Panzer-Division. An aristocratic cavalryman, he survived the war and later served in the Bundeswehr. In retirement he became heavily involved in equestrian sports, helping to train the Canadian team for the 1964 Tokyo Olympics.

Major elements (1944)
Panzer-Regiment 100
Panzergrenadier-Regiment 125
Panzergrenadier-Regiment 192
Panzeraufklärungs-Abteilung 200
Panzer-Pionier-Abteilung 220
Sturmgeschütz-Abteilung 200
Panzer-Artillerie-Regiment 155

Divisional commanders
Generalmajor Johannes Streich (February–July 1941)
Generalmajor Johann von Ravenstein (July–November 1941)
Oberstleutnant Gustav-Georg Knabe (November 1941)
Generalleutnant Karl Bottcher (December 1941–February 1942)
Generalmajor Georg von Bismarck (February–August 1942)
Oberst Carl-Hans Lungershausen (September 1942)
Generalleutnant Heinz von Randow (September–December 1942)
Generalleutnant Hans-Georg Hildebrandt (January–March 1943)
Generalmajor Heinrich-Hermann von Hülsen (April–May 1943)
Generalleutnant Feuchtinger (May 1943–January 1944)
Generalmajor Oswin Grolig (January–March 1944)
Generalleutnant Franz Westhoven (March–May 1944)

Generalleutnant Feuchtinger (May 1944–January 1945)
Oberst Helmut Zollenkopf (January–February 1945)
Generalmajor Marcks (February–April 1945)

Special insignia
None.

24. PANZER-DIVISION

This formation traced its origins to 1.(Ostpreussische) Kavallerie-Brigade in 1921. On the outbreak of war in September 1939 the brigade saw action in the Polish campaign, advancing with 3. Armee via Myseinice and Frankovo and crossing the Narev and Bug rivers in the drive to Warsaw. It was expanded to divisional status in December 1939 as **1. Kavallerie-Division**.[4] In the Western campaign of 1940 this horsed formation advanced into Friesland in the northern Netherlands against fairly weak opposition until it ran up against the Dutch fortress of Kornwerderzand, which was supported by Dutch gunboats on the Waddenzee; however, the Dutch surrender saved the division from the possibility of heavy casualties in any attempted assault. Thereafter the 1st Cavalry Division moved into France, advancing with XXXVIII Korps of 4. Armee over the Somme and the Seine, and reaching La Rochelle by the time of the French capitulation on 23 June. After a period in France on occupation duties the division was withdrawn to the east to prepare for Operation 'Barbarossa'.

During the invasion of Russia in summer 1941 the 1st Cavalry Division served with XXIV Korps in Army Group Centre, protecting the right flank of Guderian's 2nd Panzer Group during the crossing of the Dnieper and the drive on Smolensk, and fighting around the Bryansk Pocket. The horsemen were particularly successful against by-passed Soviet units counter-attacking from the northern fringe of the Pripet Marshes. Before the onset of winter 1941 it was withdrawn from the Eastern Front and moved to France, for re-organisation as the 24. Panzer-Division in November.

The new division was attached to 6. Armee under Generaloberst von Paulus and took part in the fateful 1942 summer offensive to the Volga. It perished at Stalingrad with the rest of 6. Armee, its pitiful remnants passing into Soviet captivity in March 1943.

The division was re-formed shortly thereafter; and after a brief spell in Northern Italy the new formation moved to the Eastern Front, where it suffered heavy losses in the ferocious battles around Kiev in November 1943. In March 1944, 24. Panzer-Division took part in the relief of the Cherkassy Pocket, the gallantry of its troops earning it a formal mention in despatches. During the German collapse of that summer the division made a fighting withdrawal through Poland and into Hungary, where it counter-attacked west of Debrecen, but later took very heavy casualties in the defence of Kecskemet. In the final weeks of the war the remnants of 24. Panzer-Division were fighting in north-east Prussia, where they went into Soviet captivity in May 1945.

4 See MAA 361, *Axis Cavalry in World War II*

(*continued on page 33*)

1: Schütze, Inf-Regt 'Grossdeutschland', 1939
2: Feldwebel, Feldgendarmerietrupp 'GD', 1941
3: Unteroffizier, Flak-Abteilung 'GD', 1943–44

A

1: Hauptmann, PzGren-Regt 'Feldherrnhalle', 1943
2: Funker, PzGren-Div 'Feldherrnhalle', 1943–44
3: Obergefreiter, Pz-Abteilung 'Feldherrnhalle', 1943

B

1: Hauptmann, Inf-Regt 119 'List', 57. Inf-Div, 1943
2: Major, PzGren-Div 'Brandenburg', late 1944
3: Unteroffizier, Gren-Regt 134, 44. ReichsGren-Div
   'Hoch und Deutschmeister', 1944

1: Leutnant, Sturmartillerie,
   116. Pz-Div, 1944
2: Feldwebel, Pz-Regt 22,
   21. Pz-Div, 1944
3: Unteroffizier, PzGren-Lehr-Regt
   901, (130.) Pz-Lehr-Div, 1944

D

1: Feldwebel, schwere Panzer-Abteilung 503, 1944
2: Leutnant Otto Carius, sPz-Abt 502
3: Major Erich Schmidt, sPz-Abt 507
4: Major Willi Jähde, sPz-Abt 502

E

1: Leutnant, Kav-Regt 5
   'Feldmarschall von Mackensen', 1945
2: Oberreiter, Kav-Regt 5
   'Feldmarschall von Mackensen', 1945
3: Feldwebel, Pz-Regt 24, 24. Pz-Div, 1943

1: Feldwebel of Panzertruppe, Führer-Begleit-Brigade, 1944
2: Panzergrenadier, Führer-Grenadier-Division, 1945
3: Feldwebel, Wachbataillon Berlin, c.1943

1: Feldwebel, Gebirgsjäger-Regt 138, 3. Gebirgs-Div, c.1942

2: Generaloberst Eduard Dietl, 1943

3: Gefreiter, 5. Gebirgs-Div, 1943

Major Josef Rettemeier of 24. Panzer-Division, a veteran of the North African campaign, wears the *Afrika* commemorative cuffband on the left sleeve of his black vehicle uniform with that formation's special golden-yellow piping.

Main elements
Panzer-Regiment 24
Panzergrenadier-Regiment 21
Panzergrenadier-Regiment 26
Panzerartillerie-Regiment 89
Panzeraufklärungs-Abteilung 24
Heeres-Flak-Abteilung 283
Panzerpionier-Bataillon 40

Divisional commanders
Generalleutnant Kurt Feldt (November 1941–April 1942)
Generalmajor Bruno Ritter von Hauenschild (April–September 1942)
Generalleutnant Arno von Lenski (September 1942–January 1943)
Generalleutnant Maximillian Reichs-Freiherr von Edelsheim (March 1943–August 1944)
Generalmajor Gustav Adolf von Nostitz-Wallwitz (August 1944–March 1945)
Generalleutnant Rudolf von Knebel Döberitz (March–May 1945)
(Throughout the war the division's officers included a higher than usual proportion of aristocrats, reflecting the old cavalry tradition.)

Special insignia
While no special badges were worn, this formation was unique among the Panzer divisions in its visible reflection of the cavalry roots from which it sprang. Instead of the regulation rose-pink of the Panzertruppe, all uniform and insignia piping – to the peaked service cap, field cap, and the shoulder straps, collar patches and collar of the black vehicle uniform jacket – was in the cavalry's golden-yellow Waffenfarbe. Within other Panzer divisions the crews of armoured reconnaissance vehicles were authorised cavalry yellow Waffenfarbe; but the 24th was unique in that this colour was also worn by its tank crews.

(130.) PANZER-LEHR-DIVISION

This relatively 'new' division, formed only on 30 December 1943, was created from some of the best and most experienced Panzer soldiers in the German Army. The title 'Lehr' indicates an élite evaluation and demonstration unit. At the suggestion of the Generalinspekteur der Panzertruppe, Generaloberst Heinz Guderian, the Panzer-Lehr-Division was built around a strong cadre of men who had served as instructors in the Army's various tank training schools, most of whom had already seen extensive combat on the Eastern Front. Guderian also ensured that these highly experienced troops were issued with only the best equipment, including a full complement of the excellent PzKw V Panther tank, often in short supply. He also saw to it that command was given to one of his most trusted subordinates, Generalleutnant Fritz Bayerlein, who had proved himself in North Africa under Rommel. The division was fully motorised, and its infantry were true Panzergrenadiers, all transported in armoured half-tracks instead of the more usual mix of half-tracks and 'softskin' trucks.

By the spring of 1944 the formation was at full strength, and its first operational posting was to Hungary; but it remained there only briefly before being transferred to France in preparation for the anticipated Allied invasion. On 6 June 1944 the division was in the area around Paris, under the control of I SS-Panzer-Korps; it was immediately ordered to move towards the coast, but under skies ruled by the Allies the journey took two full days. By the time Panzer-Lehr reached the vicinity of Caen on 8 June it had already lost over 200 vehicles to the Allied fighter-bombers before it even saw action. The division went into combat the next day, only to find that part of its assigned area of operations had already been taken by the British 8th Armoured Brigade. Panzer-Lehr attacked, but the situation had already deteriorated to the extent that the operation was called off because of enemy pressure on the division's flanks; however, they successfully fended off further British attacks around Tilly, operating alongside SS Panzer units.

By 11 June it had become clear that the original task which the division had been allocated – to destroy the Allied bridgehead – was no longer feasible; and Panzer-Lehr, with the rest of I SS-Panzer-Korps, went onto the defensive. For the next two days the division resisted strong enemy attacks which were supported by heavy naval gunfire from warships lying off the coast. On 13 June British units penetrated Panzer-Lehr's flanks, but were thrown back by a counter-attack at Villers-Bocage, the scene of the historic action by Waffen-SS Tiger tank ace Michael Wittmann. The arrival of 2. Panzer-Division in the area in mid-June eased the pressure on Panzer-Lehr slightly, but the division had already suffered almost 20 per cent losses.

The division's darkest day came in the second half of July 1944. On the 25th a massed USAAF bomber attack saw over 4,000 tons of bombs dropped on Panzer-Lehr's positions in preparation for the US break-out offensive in southern Normandy, Operation 'Cobra'. The divisional commander Gen. Bayerlein described the resulting appearance of the area as a heavily cratered moonscape; and it was estimated that up to 70 per cent of Panzer-Lehr's personnel were killed, wounded, or temporarily disabled due to concussion and shock.

Panzer-Lehr took part in the general withdrawal from Normandy in late summer 1944, crossing the Seine and moving right back to the German border. In October 1944 it was completely refitted but with a reduced establishment, featuring only a single battalion of tanks rather than a two-battalion regiment. In December, Panzer-Lehr took part in the ill-fated Ardennes offensive as part of 5. Panzerarmee under Gen. von Manteuffel, fighting around the Bastogne area. When the offensive was halted Panzer-Lehr relocated to Holland, whence it gradually withdrew into Germany, fighting on the Saar and against the Remagen bridgehead. It finally surrendered to US forces in the Ruhr Pocket in April 1945.

Oberstleutnant Bruno Kahl, a highly decorated soldier who served with several prestigious formations including Panzer-Regiment 'Grossdeutschland'. He commanded Panzer-Lehr-Regiment 130, the core of the Panzer-Lehr-Division.

Main elements
Panzer-Lehr-Regiment 130
Panzergrenadier-Lehr-Regiment 901
Panzer-Artillerie-Regiment 130
Panzeraufklärungs-Lehr-Abteilung 130
Panzerjäger-Lehr-Abteilung 130
Heeres-Flak-Abteilung 331
Panzer-Pionier-Bataillon 130

Divisional commanders
Generalleutnant Fritz Bayerlein (January–June 1944)
Generalmajor Hyazinth Graf Strachwitz von Gross-Zauche und Camminetz (June–August 1944)
Oberst Rudolf Gerhardt (August–September 1944)
Oberst Paul Freiherr von Hauser (September 1944)
Generalleutnant Fritz Bayerlein (September 1944–January 1945)
Generalmajor Horst Niemack (January–April 1945)
Oberst Paul Freiherr von Hauser (April 1945)

Special insignia
The only special insignia was the letter 'L' for Lehr which was worn on the shoulder straps by all divisional personnel – embroidered in the relevant Waffenfarbe for junior ranks, stamped in white metal for senior NCO ranks (see Plate D5) and gilt metal for officers.

3. GEBIRGS-DIVISION

As with many of the German Army's mountain units, 3. Gebirgs-Division had its origins in the Austrian Army. Following the Anschluss in 1938 the Austrian 5th and 7th Divisions were amalgamated to become 3. Gebirgs-Division.

The division served in the brief Polish campaign with Heeresgruppe Süd; but although committed to the Eifel region for the forthcoming campaign in the West it saw no significant action before being chosen as one of the lead formations for the attack on Narvik during the invasion of Norway in April 1940. The mountain troopers were transported to Narvik in ships of the Kriegsmarine's destroyer flotilla; most arrived at their destination weakened by seasickness after several hours cooped up below decks on destroyers tossed about in rough seas. The Gebirgsjäger accepted the surrender of the Norwegian garrison, but were themselves isolated by the arrival of the Royal Navy, which over the course of several brief but ferocious engagements involving British destroyers and the battleship HMS *Warspite* sank the entire force of ten German destroyers.

In appalling weather conditions the mountain troops fought tenaciously to defend their perimeter against Polish, French, Norwegian and British troops. Hitler, not known for allowing his commanders to retreat, proposed the evacuation of the Gebirgsjäger, or the alternative of having them march into neutral Sweden and accept internment rather than surrender. The divisional commander, Gen. Eduard Dietl, persuaded Hitler that the mountain troopers should hold fast; by this point over 15,000 enemy troops were pressing in on his shrinking but

General Eduard Dietl, the 'Hero of Narvik' and commander of 3. Gebirgs-Division, after the award of the Oakleaves to his Knight's Cross. He wears the Narvik Shield on his upper left sleeve. See Plate H2.

stubbornly held perimeter. A few paratroopers – including volunteers from the 2. Gebirgs-Division – were dropped to reinforce Dietl's command, but the position remained precarious. Other elements of the 2nd Mountain Division struck out overland in an attempt to relieve the 3rd Division, 125 miles away. Selecting the fittest and most experienced troops for an advance force, the commander of 2. Gebirgs-Division asked his men for an all-out effort to reach their comrades. Fate was to reward Dietl's determination, however; when the relief force was still three days' march away Norway surrendered. Dietl would thereafter be fêted as the 'Hero of Narvik', but would admit that he had been on the point of conceding defeat.

In June 1941, 3. Gebirgs-Division took part in the invasion of the Soviet Union, striking north-east from Finland towards Murmansk. Denied the capture of the Soviet port, the division spent over a year in aggressive but essentially static warfare against the Red Army before being moved to the southern sector of the front. The 3rd Mountain Division ultimately formed part of 6. Armee, rebuilt after the disaster at Stalingrad, and fought in the defensive battles as the Germans withdrew from the Ukraine and into Hungary and Slovakia. It served out the last few weeks of the war in defensive operations in Silesia, where it finally surrendered to the Red Army.

Men of 3. Gebirgs-Division on the Eastern Front in 1942; the Obergefreiter with the binoculars is a veteran of the battle for Narvik as evidenced by the Narvik Shield on the left sleeve of his greatcoat. Note the Edelweiss badge on the left side of the short-visored Bergmützen caps. (Josef Charita)

Main elements
Gebirgsjäger-Regiment 138
Gebirgsjäger-Regiment 139
Gebirgs-Artillerie-Regiment 112
Gebirgs-Aufklärungs-Abteilung 12
Gebirgs-Pionier-Bataillon 82
Gebirgs-Panzerabwehr-Abteilung 48

Divisional commanders
Generaloberst Eduard Dietl (September 1939–June 1940)
General Julius Ringel (June–October 1940)
General Hans Kreysin (October 1940–August 1943)
Generalleutnant Egbert Picker (August 1943)
General Siegfried Rasp (August–September 1943)
Generalleutnant Egbert Picker (September 1943)
Generalleutnant August Wittmann (September 1943–July 1944)
Generalleutnant Paul Klatt (July 1944–May 1945)

Special insignia
The most significant piece of insignia pertinent to this division was the special Narvik campaign shield worn on the left sleeve. This award was instituted on 19 August 1940 and took the form of a silvered metal shield topped by an eagle and swastika and the legend 'Narvik'. On the shield were depicted a propeller (for the Luftwaffe), an anchor (for the Navy) and an Edelweiss (for the Gebirgsjäger), symbolising the combined effort made by all three services in the battle of Narvik.[5]

TOP **The Narvik Shield, issued in silver (actually light grey zinc) for the Luftwaffe and Army and gold for the Navy. In the case of awards to Gebirgsjäger, as here, it is mounted on a piece of field-grey backing cloth for stitching to the uniform sleeve.** ABOVE **The Mountain Troops' Edelweiss sleeve patch in a hand-embroidered officer's quality example using aluminium and gold-coloured wire.**

The divisional personnel naturally also wore the special Edelweiss insignia which identified all mountain units. The right sleeve patch consisted of a white Edelweiss flower with yellow stamens and green stem, set within a silver-grey twisted rope border with a piton at its top. This was made in both machine-embroidered and woven forms for lower ranks, and occasionally in hand-embroidered bullion thread for officers. The standard metal Edelweiss emblem was also worn on the left side of the Bergmütze.

5. GEBIRGS-DIVISION

This division had its roots in the mountains of Bavaria where most of its personnel were recruited, though its home base was at Graz, Austria. The division was formed in 1940 around a cadre element transferred from 1. Gebirgs-Division. After training in the Alps it was moved into the Balkans, taking part in the invasion of Greece and the destruction of the 'Metaxas' defence line. Almost immediately afterwards it fought its most significant battle when, in May 1941, it took part in the invasion of the island of Crete.

The 5th Mountain had not been one of the formations originally intended for this operation, but was pulled in at the last moment to make up a shortfall in available troops. From its base in Greece it was to move to Crete in stages to back up the Fallschirmjäger who would have already landed. The first wave was to be transported by the Luftwaffe in Ju52 transports to Maleme airfield as soon as it had been captured (although each plane could carry only 12 men with their full equipment, so many flights would be needed). The second wave was to be transported by sea, also to Maleme; for this purpose the divisional commander, Generalleutnant Julius 'Papa' Ringel, commandeered a fleet of more than 60 small Greek fishing vessels (caiques). Disaster struck when the caiques were intercepted on 19 May and sunk by warships of the Royal Navy; of the two full battalions being transported, only 52 men made it to Crete.

The Gebirgsjäger transported by air found their planes coming under heavy fire as they landed, from New Zealand troops who still held the heights overlooking Maleme. Each squad was forced to dash for cover as soon as they exited the aircraft, which had to turn around and take off again immediately, still under fire and avoiding the wrecked aircraft which littered the runway. Eventually, by mid-day on 22 May, a full battalion had been landed, and they began to first secure and then gradually to expand their perimeter.

The troops at Maleme were formed into three Kampfgruppen. One Gebirgsjäger battle group would defend Maleme itself; the second, predominantly Fallschirmjäger, would defend the eastern approaches to the town and airfield; while the third, another Gebirgsjäger group, would attack the enemy positions overlooking Maleme. The latter group made good progress until they reached Modion, where they ran into stubborn resistance from New Zealand troops. In combat skills and determination the opponents were evenly matched, and the Germans took significant casualties before finally driving the defenders off the heights overlooking Maleme. With the airfield now safe from enemy fire there was a rapid increase in the rate of reinforcement.

The division pushed on towards Galatas where a combined attack by Gebirgsjäger and Fallschirmjäger once again successfully overcame the New Zealanders, but only after heavy fighting. With substantial German reinforcements now available the tide had finally turned against the defenders, and 5. Gebirgs-Division continued to pursue the retreating British and Commonwealth troops through the mountains to the ports from which their remnants were finally evacuated.

After their successful involvement on Crete, the division moved to the Eastern Front in March 1942, being thrown into the festering swamps of the Volkhov region in northern Russia to prevent the escape of large numbers of Soviet troops caught in the Volkhov Pocket. The enemy carried out many brave but pointless head-on attacks in an attempt to break through the German encirclement, and suffered extremely heavy losses in the process; over 33,000 Soviet prisoners were eventually taken. The division was then tasked with hunting down the large groups of Soviet stragglers, still heavily armed, who had taken to the dense forests in this region.

In the summer of 1943 the Soviets launched a major counter-offensive, which saw the division severely battered and fragmented. Despite their losses the weakened Gebirgsjäger fought with great determination – at one point a single battalion was holding off three entire Soviet regiments, in terrain ill-suited for defence. The 5th Mountain Division was eventually relieved in July 1943 and transferred to warmer climes, moving to Italy as part of 10. Armee. Here it took part in the battles to the south of Rome and the defence of the Gothic Line before being pulled back to the Franco-Italian border. It eventually surrendered to US forces at Turin in May 1945.

Main elements

Gebirgsjäger-Regiment 85
Gebirgsjäger-Regiment 100
Gebirgs-Artillerie-Regiment 95
Gebirgs-Aufklärungs-Abteilung 95
Gebirgs-Pionier-Bataillon 95
Genirgs-Panzerjäger-Abteilung 95

Divisional commanders

General Julius Ringel (November 1940–February 1944)
Generalleutnant Max Schrank (February 1944–January 1945)
Generalmajor Hans Steets (January–May 1945)

Special insignia

Apart from the regulation distinctions of the Mountain Troops, the 5. Gebirgs-Division unofficially adopted a special badge worn on the left side of the Bergmütze beside the Edelweiss. In the form of a stylised white metal chamois mountain antelope standing on a triple mountain peak, this was known as the 'Gams'.[6]

The Edelweiss, symbol of the mountain troops:
TOP **White metal cap badge with gold-coloured painted stamens.**
CENTRE **The machine-embroidered version of the sleeve patch, in golden-yellow, white and pale green with a silver-grey 'rope and piton'.**
BELOW **The woven variant, still on its backing strip.**

6 See MAA 365 *World War II German Battle Insignia* Plate H

THE TIGER TANK BATTALIONS

In the 60 years since its first appearance on the battlefield the PzKw VI Tiger tank[7] has achieved a status which can only be described as legendary. When it first rolled off the production line in 1942 the Tiger was the most powerful armoured fighting vehicle in existence. Its frontal armour was virtually impervious to all known anti-tank weapons, and its 8.8cm gun was capable of destroying all known enemy tanks well before they came within the effective range of their own main armament. It is in this sense, of employing an outstanding weapons system which achieved remarkable results, that the Tiger tank units may properly be considered an élite.

Tigers were extremely expensive to produce in terms of material and manpower resources, and were carefully husbanded. Although in the early days of its combat service several élite divisions were allocated their own Tiger units (e.g. 'Grossdeutschland', the Luftwaffe's 'Hermann Göring' Division, and the three premier Waffen-SS Panzer divisions), as a general rule they came to be deployed at Corps, Army or even Army Group level in specially formed Heavy Tank Battalions (schwere Panzer-Abteilungen). The higher command would then decide which sector of the front most needed these scarce assets, shifting them from area to area to deal with crises. A typical schwere Panzer-Abteilung had a headquarters element and three companies of Tigers, each nominally 14 tanks strong, plus service and support elements. In some cases, particularly during the early days of its use, there were insufficient Tigers to fully equip the heavy battalions, and a company of lighter tanks such as PzKw IIIs were substituted.

The following Army Heavy Tank Battalions were formed:

schwere Panzer-Abteilung 501

Formed in 1942. One full company of this unit was shipped to Tunisia in November 1942, seeing action against the Allies at Tebourba and Hamra, and in February 1943 around Kasserine. The elements in North Africa were forced to surrender along with the rest of the Axis forces in May 1943 after fierce combat in the Medjerda Valley; but the battalion was re-formed around the companies which had remained in Europe, on occupation duty in France. Fully up to strength, it was sent to the Eastern Front and was immediately involved in defensive actions around Vitebsk and Gorodok. The battalion was refitted with the even heavier Tiger II ('Königstiger') in July 1944. Thereafter it fought on the defensive as the German armies retreated through Poland, seeing particularly heavy fighting at Radom and Kleice. In December 1944,

Major Willy Jähde, commander of schwere Panzer-Abteilung 502, wearing the sheepskin over-jacket popular with some Tiger crews on the Eastern Front – see Plate E.

Leutnant Otto Carius, commander of 2 Kompanie/schwere Panzer-Abteilung 502, wearing an optional private purchase white summer tunic. This photo was taken while he was still recuperating from wounds received in the action for which he was decorated with the Oakleaves to his Knight's Cross – cf Plate E. He was shot five times while carrying out a reconnaisance on foot, but recovered to return to front-line duty.

sPz-Abt 501 was disbanded and used to form the new **sPz-Abt 424**, which was attached to XXIV Panzerkorps; this was little more than a renaming exercise, as the unit remained in the same sector of the front under the same commander. The battalion was finally completely disbanded in February 1945.

Unit commanders:

Major Erich Löwe (Sept–Dec 1943); Oberstleutnant von Legat (Jan–Aug 1944); Major Saemisch (Aug 1944–Feb 1945)

Unit insignia:

An emblem depicting a prowling tiger was painted on some of the unit's tanks. In some cases, though prohibited by this time in the war, unit personnel, principally officers, wore the gilt numerals '501' on their shoulder straps.

schwere Panzer-Abteilung 502

Formed in August 1942. Tanks from this unit were the first Tigers to see action on the Eastern Front when the unit was committed to combat near Leningrad, but were at first of dubious value; many suffered mechanical breakdowns or bogged down in marshy terrain, several being captured almost intact by the Soviets. The Tigers were committed without infantry support, allowing the enemy to attack their more vulnerable flanks, and some were lost simply due to their tracks being damaged by enemy infantry. The unit remained on the northern sector of the front until the great Soviet counter-offensives of 1944, when it withdrew into Kurland. In late 1944 it fought on the defensive around Memel and Königsberg. The unit was re-formed in early 1945 as **sPz-Abt 511**, equipped with the Tiger II. By the time it finally surrendered to the Soviets on 9 May 1945 this single battalion had recorded a total of some 2,000 Soviet armoured vehicles destroyed.

Unit commanders:

Hauptmann Arthur Wollschläger (Nov 1942–Feb 1943); Major Richter (Feb–July 1943); Hauptmann Erich Schmidt (July–Aug 1943); Hauptmann Lange (Aug–Oct 1943); Major Willi Jähde (Oct 1943–March 1944); Major Schwaner (Apr–Aug 1944); Hauptmann von Foerstner (Aug 1944–Jan 1945)

Unit insignia:

The emblem of a woolly mammoth with large curved tusks was painted on some of the unit's vehicles.

schwere Panzer-Abteilung 503

This battalion was formed in spring 1942. It had originally been destined for North Africa but in the event was committed to action on the southern sector of the Eastern Front, where it helped to cover the German retreat from the area around Stalingrad. It took part in the great tank battles at Kursk in July 1943 before being attached to Panzer-Regiment Bäke, with which it fought with great élan in the battles around Cherkassy, destroying over 260 enemy tanks in one action over five days. It remained with the regiment until April 1944, when it was withdrawn to the West for refitting with the Tiger II. It was caught up in the battles following the Allied landings in Normandy in June 1944, and many of its tanks were lost to enemy fighter-bombers and naval gunfire. In September, fully refitted, it returned to the Eastern Front to take part in the defence of Hungary. In January 1945 it was renamed as **sPz-Abt 'Feldherrnhalle'** and attached to the Panzergrenadier division of that name, with which it was destroyed in the final battles on the Eastern Front.

Unit commanders:
Oberstleutnant Post (May 1942–Jan 1943); Oberstleutnant Hoheisel (Jan–May 1943); Hauptmann Clemens Graf von Kageneck (May 1943–Feb 1944); Hauptmann Rolf Fromme (Feb–Dec 1944); Hauptmann Nordewin von Diest-Koerber (Dec 1944–Jan 1945)

Unit insignia:
The unit emblem painted on some of its vehicles consisted of a tiger's head. Some personnel also wore a small white metal badge in the shape of a King Tiger tank on the left side of the field cap.

Feldwebel Albert Kerscher, one of the highly decorated NCO Tiger commanders from schwere Panzer-Abteilung 502.

schwere Panzer-Abteilung 504

Formed in February 1943. Elements of this battalion were committed in Tunisia, seeing action around Maknassy and Medjerda. The remainder of the battalion, located in Sicily, was withdrawn onto the Italian mainland after resisting the Allied invasion of the island. It then moved to Holland for a refit before returning to Italy in June 1944. It subsequently took part in operations to contain the Allied bridgehead at Anzio, and also fought in the defence of the Gothic Line facing British troops. It remained in Italy until the German surrender in May 1945.

Unit commanders:
Major August Seidensticker (Feb–May 1943); Hauptmann Kühn (Nov 1943–Sept 1944); Major Nill (Sept 1944–May 1945)

schwere Panzer-Abteilung 505

Formed in January 1943, the battalion first saw serious action at the battle of Kursk that July when it was attached to 9. Armee on the northern flank of the salient. It subsequently came under command of Heeresgruppe Mitte, fighting at Smolensk. Re-equipped with Tiger IIs in late summer 1944, it was committed to action once again in the defensive battles for East Prussia, providing heavy support to 24. and 25. Panzer-Divisions. It was heavily involved in the defence of the Narev bridgehead, remaining in East Prussia until the end of the war.

Unit commanders:
Major Bernhard Sauvant (Feb–Aug 1943); Hauptmann von Karlowitz (Aug–Sept 1943); Hauptmann Werner Freiherr von Beschwitz (Sept 1943–Nov 1944); Major Senfft von Pilsach (Nov 1944–Apr 1945)

Unit insignia:
An emblem depicting a charging armoured knight on horseback, armed with a lance, was painted on the turret side of some of the battalion's tanks.

schwere Panzer-Abteilung 506

Formed in July 1943, this unit first fought in the defensive battles along the Dnieper River as part of Heeresgruppe Mitte; it saw action at Lemburg, Tarna and Krivoi-Rog. Withdrawn from the front in August 1944, it returned to Germany to refit with the Tiger II. In September it was committed to action at Oosterbeek following the Allied airborne landings at Arnhem. In November 1944 it received – unusually for a Tiger unit – a fourth company. It saw action in the

Major Clemens Graf von Kageneck, commander of schwere Panzer-Abteilung 503. Many members of the German nobility served in armoured units.

Hauptmann Wolfgang Koltermann, commander of 3 Kompanie/schwere Panzer-Abteilung 507. Koltermann was of very diminutive stature, but his size was belled by ⁹ ˢⁱᶻᵉ bravery.

Ardennes offensive before fighting in the defence of the Ruhr, where it was encircled and forced to surrender to US forces in April 1945.

Unit commanders:

Major Gerhard Willig (July–Oct 1943); Major Lange (Oct 1943–Jan 1945); Hauptmann Heiligenstadt (Jan–Feb 1945); Hauptmann von Römer (Feb–April 1945)

Unit insignia:

Painted on some vehicles was a letter 'W' for Willig, over which leans a Tiger holding a red shield emblazoned with a white cross.

schwere Panzer-Abteilung 507

Formed in September 1943, this battalion was first committed to action in March 1944 on the Eastern Front, where it saw heavy defensive fighting at Tarnopol, Vitebsk and on the Narev River front. After refitting with the Tiger II in February 1945 it returned to the Eastern Front, fighting in defence of Czechoslovakia in the closing months of the war. Having lost all its Tigers in action, the battalion tried to make its way west to surrender to US forces but was intercepted and captured by the Soviets.

Unit commanders:

Major Erich Schmidt (Sept 1943–Aug 1944); Hauptmann Fritz Schöck (Aug 1944–May 1945)

Unit insignia:

The unit emblem painted on some vehicles was a shield showing a blacksmith fashioning a sword on an anvil.

schwere Panzer-Abteilung 508

Formed in August 1943, this unit was sent to the Italian Front, where it suffered heavy casualties at Anzio and Nettuno. It fought throughout the subsequent retreat up Italy, eventually being disbanded in February 1945 when all its tanks had been destroyed or disabled. The remaining personnel were returned to Germany for re-allocation to other units.

Unit commanders:

Major Hudel (Jan–May 1944); Hauptmann Stelter (Aug 1944–Feb 1945)

Unit insignia:

A black bison within a black outline shield is recorded as the vehicle emblem.

schwere Panzer-Abteilung 509

Formed in September 1943, this unit was first used on the Eastern Front, seeing heavy action at Kirovograd, Zhitomir and Kiev. In late 1943 it was briefly attached to 2. SS-Panzer-Division 'Das Reich' during actions at Kaminets-Podolsk. In 1944 it was heavily committed to defensive fighting in the southern sector following the launch of the Soviet summer offensive, once again going into action at Kiev and Zhitomir. In late 1944 it returned to Germany where, at the Sennelager tank training grounds, it was re-equipped with Tiger IIs. In January 1945 it was sent to Hungary as part of IV SS-

Panzer-Korps, and was gradually forced back into Austria where it surrendered to US forces. By this point it had no tanks left, its vehicles consisting of just one amphibious VW Schwimmwagen, one Funkwagen and one truck.

Unit commanders:

Hauptmann Hannibal von Lüttichau (Aug–Nov 1943); Major Gierka (Nov 1943–Feb 1944); Hauptmann Radtke (Feb–March 1944); Hauptmann Hans-Jürgen Burmester (March 1944–Feb 1945); Hauptmann Dr König (Feb–May 1945)

Unit insignia:

A tiger's head on a shield is recorded as a vehicle emblem.

schwere Panzer-Abteilung 510

Formed in June 1944, this unit had reached the northern sector of the Eastern Front within a month. In East Prussia the battalion was divided, part being sent to support 14. Panzer-Division and the remainder to 30. Infanterie-Division. The elements operating with 14. Panzer-Division saw heavy combat in the Kurland peninsula in early 1945. In March two companies were withdrawn to Kassel in Germany and the rest, with 13 remaining Tiger I tanks, were assigned to 11. Panzer-Division. The last Tiger was lost on 8 May, and the battalion surrendered along with the other survivors of the fierce Kurland battles. This was the only schwere Panzer-Abteilung never to have been equipped with the Tiger II, all of its tanks being late model Tiger Is.

Hauptmann Walter Scherff, commander of 3 Kompanie/ schwere Panzer-Abteilung 503, wearing the *Feldbluse mit Vorstössen* or 'piped field service tunic'. This incorporated some features of the *Waffenrock*: piping in branch colour round the collar and cuffs and down the front edge, and collar *Litzen* mounted on patches of branch colour.

THE PLATES

A1: Schütze, Infanterie-Regiment 'Grossdeutschland', 1939

This private wears the special pre-war parade dress uniform; although this was never generally issued, stocks were stored for issue after the anticipated successful conclusion to the war. Note the special cuff design, quite different to that on normal Waffenrock parade tunics; and the unique collar patches with much longer silver braid *Litzen* than was normal. His shoulder straps bear the regimental 'GD' ciphers embroidered in the white Waffenfarbe of the infantry; and on his right cuff is the first pattern machine-woven *Grossdeutschland* cuffband in silver Gothic script on dark green. The white-piped trousers are in stone-grey.

A2: Feldwebel, Feldgendarmerietrupp 'Grossdeutschland', 1941

This NCO from the divisional military police troop wears the standard M1936 Feldbluse with orange military police piping to the shoulder straps and 'lights' on the collar patches, and the orange police-style wreathed eagle badge on his upper

Major Otto Ernst Remer of the 'Grossdeutschland', shown here after the award of the Oakleaves to his Knight's Cross. He was ultimately promoted to Generalmajor and commanded the Führer-Begleit-Division. Remer was instrumental in suppressing the attempted seizure of power in Berlin following the abortive assassination attempt on Hitler on 20 July 1944.

This Unteroffizier wears the regulation *Feldherrnhalle* cuffband, but not the SA-Kampfrune insignia on the shoulder straps; cf Plate B. (Josef Charita)

left sleeve. The senior NCOs' 'GD' cipher in stamped white metal is pinned between the rank 'pips' on his shoulder straps, which are trimmed – like his collar – with silver-grey *Tresse* braid. The machine-woven *Feldgendarmerie* cuffband is worn on the lower left sleeve, and the third pattern Sütterlin script *Grossdeutschland* cuffband on the right. Of special interest is the unique gorget used by this unit; an unofficial but tolerated affectation, it was the standard Feldgendarmerie pattern with the addition of a blackened plate bearing the unit cipher 'GD'. His equipment includes a holstered P08 pistol, a mapcase and a field torch.

A3: Unteroffizier, Flak-Abteilung 'Grossdeutschland', 1943–44

The typical appearance of a junior squad leader in the second half of the war. This Unteroffizier wears the M1943 Feldbluse with plain field-grey collar, and plain grey *Litzen*; an M1942 steel helmet with a roughened paint finish; and ankle boots with canvas gaiters. On his right sleeve is the final pattern copperplate script *Grossdeutschland* cuffband; on his shoulder straps, the divisional cipher in the red Waffenfarbe of the Flakartillerie; and on his upper right sleeve the red winged shell badge special to this unit. The men of the anti-tank unit had to be prepared to defend their gun positions against infantry attack, and this NCO has full rifleman's equipment, with an entrenching spade thrust into his belt and his Seitengewehr 84/98 bayonet fixed.

Inset A4: 'Grossdeutschland' shoulder strap cipher in senior NCOs' stamped white metal format.

B1: Hauptmann, Panzergrenadier-Regiment 'Feldherrnhalle', 1943

This captain from the armoured infantry regiment of the Panzergrenadier-Division formed in 1943 round the nucleus of Infanterie-Regiment 271 is in field service dress. He wears the officer's quality version of an M1936 Feldbluse, privately tailored but maintaining some of the basic features of the enlisted ranks' version. His shoulder straps, collar patches and cap bear the grass-green piping of a Panzergrenadier, the former with the pin-on gilt metal *Kampfrune* insignia of this division. On his left cuff is the *Feldherrnhalle* cuffband in woven aluminium wire on brown fabric. His decorations include both classes of the Iron Cross, the bronze Tank Battle Badge of the Panzergrenadiers, and a Wound Badge.

B2: Funker, Panzergrenadier-Division 'Feldherrnhalle', 1943–44

An enlisted signaller from a 'Feldherrnhalle' headquarters company wears a late war M1943 Feldbluse in coarse field-grey wool with a high shoddy content. His shoulder straps are piped in the lemon-yellow Waffenfarbe of the signals branch; although examples with the runic insignia embroidered in Waffenfarbe existed, photographs show that many junior ranks simply pinned the white metal NCOs' version on to plain straps. He wears a 'BeVo'-woven example of the *Feldherrnhalle* cuffband in grey silk thread on brown. His helmet is the M1942 with flared rim, by now devoid of insignia decals and field-camouflaged with mud. Again, he carries full rifle equipment including a couple of Stielhandgranate 24 stick grenades and a 250-round machine gun ammunition box; no matter what their specialist function, under the conditions of the Russian Front all personnel needed to be able to fight as infantrymen.

B3: Obergefreiter, Panzer-Abteilung 'Feldherrnhalle', 1943

The standard early wartime black Panzer vehicle uniform is worn by this junior NCO from the tank battalion of the newly formed Panzergrenadier-Division. The *Feldherrnhalle* cuffband in artificial silk weave is worn on the left sleeve, and the embroidered *Kampfrune* insignia on the black wool shoulder straps in the rose-pink Waffenfarbe of armoured troops. The cuffband and shoulder ciphers appear not to have been as universally worn within this formation as was the case in 'Grossdeutschland' units.

Inset B4: The political-style Fahne of the SA-Standarte, also carried by the Army unit. **B5:** The *Kampfrune* cipher in stamped white metal, worn by senior NCOs but also by many junior ranks due to shortages of embroidered shoulder straps. **B6:** The special SA-style standard bearer's gorget worn by 'Feldherrnhalle' units.

C1: Hauptmann, Infanterie-Regiment 119 'List', 57. Infanterie-Division, 1943

Apart from the regimental cuffband on his left sleeve, embroidered in 'copperplate' script, this captain from Infanterie-Regiment 'List' is fairly typical of the appearance of an infantry officer in the second half of the war. He wears an altered enlisted man's Feldbluse, more appropriate for combat wear than an officer's tunic, with the service dress Dienstmütze peaked cap, breeches and regulation officer's boots. A highly decorated soldier, he wears at his throat the Knight's Cross with Oakleaves.

C2: Major, Panzergrenadier-Division 'Brandenburg', late 1944

One of the rarest élite insignia was the *Brandenburg* cuffband. Here it is worn by an officer from one of the two Jäger (Rifles) regiments of Panzergrenadier-Division 'Brandenburg' in the closing stages of the war. On the upper right sleeve is the cloth patch showing an oakleaf spray, the traditional emblem of the light infantry. By this stage in the war the Brandenburg Division was operating in a conventional infantry role, though a proportion of veterans of the early commando operations – like this officer – were still with the unit. He has been decorated progressively with the Iron Cross 1st Class, the German Cross in Gold, and the Knight's Cross with Oakleaves, and also wears the black Wound Badge and the Infantry Assault Badge.

C3: Unteroffizier, Grenadier-Regiment 134, 44. Reichsgrenadier-Division 'Hoch und Deutschmeister', 1944

A seasoned Eastern Front veteran, this NCO cleaning the action of an MG34 squad light machine gun wears late war combat uniform of the M1943 tunic, ankle boots and canvas gaiters. Most high quality leather equipment from the first part of the war had by this stage been replaced with utilitarian webbing, though this soldier has managed to retain a black leather belt. His shoulder straps bear the coloured metal 'Stalingrad Cross' emblem commemorating the destruction of the former 44. Inf-Div in that battle. We illustrate on his left sleeve the cuffband *Hoch- und Deutschmeister* embroidered in grey Gothic script on a black background; its use is somewhat speculative – despite assertions from some veterans no photographic evidence to support its wear has yet come to light.

Inset C4: The Stalingrad Cross.

D1: Leutnant, Sturmartillerie, 116. Panzer-Division, 1944

This armoured assault gun troop commander of a unit from 116. Panzer-Division during the Normandy battles wears the field-grey version of the special Panzer uniform as issued to Sturmgeschütz crews. His headgear is the popular 'old style officer's field cap' or 'crusher cap', bearing on the left side of the band the small 'greyhound' emblem of the division. His shoulder straps, collar patches and cap piping show the scarlet Waffenfarbe of the artillery branch.

D2: Feldwebel, Panzer-Regiment 22, 21. Panzer-Division, 1944

A veteran of the North African campaign, this NCO tank commander wears the standard black Panzer trousers and has retained the popular M1938 black Panzer field cap. However, instead of the black Panzerjacke he wears the lightweight field-grey denim fatigue version with a large external pocket – this was adopted by many troops during the warm summer months. On his left cuff is the campaign cuffband *Afrika*, rarely seen on the Panzer jacket as the majority of Africa veterans went into captivity in Tunisia in May 1943; this man was presumably absent on detached depot duties or convalescent leave, and later joined the re-formed division.

D3: Unteroffizier, Panzergrenadier-Lehr-Regiment 901, Panzer-Lehr-Division, 1944

This unit was known for the adoption of the field-grey Panzer-type uniform by its grenadiers. His steel helmet has a camouflaged cloth drawstring cover in the usual 'Zeltbahn pattern'. The shoulder straps bear the 'L' insignia of the Lehr units; normally this would be worn in conjunction with others to indicate the branch, e.g. 'PL' for Panzerjäger-Lehr, etc, but in the case of this division the 'L' was worn alone. The cipher is embroidered, and the shoulder straps and outer edges of the collar patches are piped in the grass-green of the Panzergrenadiers. He has been awarded the Iron Cross 2nd Class (see buttonhole ribbon), the black Wound Badge, and the bronze Panzergrenadier version of the Tank Battle Badge. As a squad leader he carries the 9mm Erma MP40

Oberleutnant Max Wirsching, commander of 2 Kompanie/schwere Panzer-Abteilung 507; cf Plate E. This Tiger tank officer wears the gilt unit number '507' on his shoulder straps, and the Honour Roll Clasp of the Army on the ribbon of the Iron Cross in his buttonhole.

sub-machine gun and wears its triple magazine pouches.

Inset D4: The 116. Pz Div 'Windhund'. **D5:** The 'L' cipher of the Panzer-Lehr-Div, in white metal.

E1: Feldwebel, schwere Panzer-Abteilung 503, 1944

The central figure of this plate represents a typical Tiger crewman in 1944. His uniform is the standard black Panzerbekleidung with M1943 Einheitsfeldmütze. On the side of his cap is a small white metal badge representing a 'King Tiger' tank as adopted by men of this battalion. His shoulder straps show the battalion number in white metal numerals; although the use of such insignia had long since been discontinued, a few individuals continued to wear them throughout the war, and the 500-series would have been a proud sign of service with the Tiger battalions.

The other images on this plate show some of the variations of appearance noted in Tiger tank units:

E2: A Luftwaffe-style black field cap, lacking the front 'scallop' to the flap usually associated with Army caps, and also lacking

A Gefreiter on leave from Infanterie-Regiment 'List', with the regimental cuffband on his left sleeve, poses proudly with his young child; cf Plate C. (Robert Noss)

A fine, rare example of a cavalry officer's 'crusher' cap.
It features cavalry golden-yellow piping and the metal
death's-head emblem worn by Kavallerie-Regiment 5;
cf Plate F. (Francois Saez)

the cockade in national colours, was regularly worn by
Leutnant Otto Carius, a Tiger 'ace' from schwere Panzer-
Abteilung 502.

E3: An unusual variant of the M1943 officer's field cap was
worn by some personnel of schwere Panzer-Abteilung 507;
not only the crown bore aluminium piping, but also the top
edge of the scalloped front portion of the side flaps. In
this study of Major Erich Schmidt the national cockade is
either missing, or hidden by the deep two-button flap.

E4: Some members of Tiger units took to wearing sheepskin
overjackets during winter months on the Eastern Front.
Major Willi Jähde, commanding officer of schwere Panzer-
Abteilung 502, was photographed wearing an example, with
the green-on-black sleeve rank insignia introduced in 1942
for all clothing which did not bear shoulder straps.

F1: Leutnant, Kavallerie-Regiment 5 'Feldmarschall von Mackensen', 1945
He wears the Dienstmütze service cap, a standard officer's
pattern M1936 type Feldbluse, riding breeches with
reinforced inner legs, and standard cavalry riding boots;
cap and tunic bear yellow cavalry Waffenfarbe distinctions.
His peaked cap bears the metal death's-head tradition
badge (originating in that of the old Prussian Life Guard
Hussars) between the Army and national insignia, and
this is repeated on his shoulder straps. On the right forearm
is the regimental cuffband *Feldmarschall v Mackensen*;
and on the upper sleeve the yellow patch adopted by
some members of 4. Kavallerie-Division in 1945.

F2: Oberreiter, Kavallerie-Regiment 5 'Feldmarschall von Mackensen', 1945
This enlisted man astride an NSU motorcycle has the
M1943 field uniform with ankle boots and canvas gaiters.
Photographs of horsed cavalry units at the end of the war
often show the old M1938 Feldmütze retained alongside
the M1943 peaked field cap; here a death's-head badge
(larger than regulation, and perhaps privately acquired?)
is pinned between the eagle and the cockade. The motif
is repeated in golden-yellow embroidery on his shoulder
straps, and he has received the regimental cuffband; these
may well have been made up locally by 'cottage industry'
in Austria. Note that this ranker wears the band on his
left sleeve.

F3: Feldwebel, Panzer-Regiment 24, 24. Panzer-Division, 1943
The cavalry roots of this formation are displayed on this
NCO tank commander's black Panzer uniform by means of
golden-yellow cavalry Waffenfarbe piping to the shoulder
straps and collar patches, and as a soutache over the
national cockade on his black Panzer Feldmütze.

G1: Feldwebel of Panzertruppe, Führer-Begleit-Brigade, 1944
This NCO serving at Führer Headquarters wears a unique
combination of insignia. As a member of an armoured unit
he wears the black Panzer uniform, but with white rather
than pink piping to his shoulder straps, collar, collar patches
and as a soutache on his field cap. He has white metal 'GD'
ciphers on his shoulder straps; on his right sleeve is the
Grossdeutschland cuffband, and on his left the cuffband
Führerhauptquartier worn by personnel actually on duty
at Hitler's headquarters. This unusual combination is known
from a handful of surviving examples of this jacket and a
few rare wartime photos.

The unique jacket worn by armoured personnel
serving with the Führer-Begleit-Brigade at Hitler's
headquarters; cf Plate G1. The piping to collar patches
and shoulder straps was white rather than the traditional
rose-pink of the armoured troops. On the left sleeve is
worn the cuffband *Führerhauptquartier*, and on the right
Grossdeutschland. (Chris Boonzaier)

General der Gebirgstruppe Julius Ringel, commander of 5. Gebirgs-Division during the battle for Crete. A popular and instantly recognisable figure, 'Papa' Ringel invariably sported a moustache and goatee beard.

G2: Panzergrenadier, Führer-Grenadier-Division, 1945

At first glance this soldier wearing the short M1944 'battledress' blouse with tapered trousers, ankle boots and canvas gaiters is fairly typical for a Panzergrenadier at this late stage of the war. What sets him apart are the 'FG' cipher embroidered in grass-green Waffenfarbe into his shoulder straps, and the *Grossdeutschland* cuffband worn on his right sleeve; this combination of insignia identifies him as a member of the short-lived Führer-Grenadier-Division. The 'FG' straps were only worn for a short period and are extremely rare. He carries a semi-automatic Kar 43 rifle and wears its canvas magazine pouches on late war webbing equipment; and his M1942 helmet has a makeshift chickenwire cover for attaching camouflage.

G3: Feldwebel, Wachbataillon Berlin, c.1943

This represents an infantry NCO of the 'Grossdeutschland' Division on rotation for duty with the Guard Battalion in Berlin. His basic M1936 service dress is that of a 'Grossdeutschland' NCO, but on his shoulder straps, instead of the normal 'GD' cipher, he displays the Gothic 'W' (for Wache, 'Guard') which was worn while serving a tour with the guard unit in the Reich capital. Such detached service was considered an honour, open only to exemplary soldiers.

Inset G4: The 'FG' cipher of the Führer-Grenadier-Division.

H1: Feldwebel, Gebirgsjäger-Regiment 138, 3. Gebirgs-Division, c.1942

This seasoned NCO of mountain infantry is a veteran of the Narvik campaign of April/May 1940. He still retains the regimental numeral '138' on his shoulder straps, though these were officially phased out after the outbreak of war. The piping round the shoulder straps and the 'lights' on the collar patches of his M1936 tunic are in the bright green of the Gebirgstruppe. On his left sleeve is the Narvik campaign shield, and on his right the Edelweis patch of the mountain troops, whose white and yellow metal cap badge is pinned to the left side of his Bergmütze. He carries full rifle equipment with a couple of M1939 'egg' grenades attached, and has been awarded the Iron Cross 2nd Class and the Infantry Assault Badge.

H2: Generaloberst Eduard Dietl, Oberbefehlshaber Lappland, 1943

One of the most charismatic figures in the Gebirgsjäger was

without doubt Gen. Eduard Dietl, in 1940 the commander of 3. Gebirgs-Division. He was a skilled mountaineer, and the rare 'Heeresbergführer' badge can be seen on his right breast pocket; a hand-embroidered Mountain Troops' Edelweiss badge is obscured here on his upper right sleeve. As well as the Narvik Shield, Knight's Cross with Oakleaves, and decorations from World War I, Dietl wears the Pilot-Observer Badge with Diamonds, an honorary award presented by Reichsmarschall Göring. Rarely will more than one photograph of Dietl show him wearing the same number of decorations; on many occasions he wore only his Knight's Cross with Oakleaves and his Narvik Shield. His stone grey breeches have the general officer's red stripes and seam piping; he normally chose to wear mountain boots with the more traditional style of puttees, wrapping all the way up to the knee, rather than riding boots or the ankle puttees. Dietl also wears a unique version of the naval dress dagger presented to him by the Kriegsmarine in commemoration of the close inter-service co-operation at Narvik. This modified piece had miniatures of the Destroyer War Badge and Mountain Troops' Edelweiss set on to the scabbard, and was suspended from regulation Army rather than Navy hanging straps. The badly damaged remains of this unique dagger were found many years after the war at the site of Dietl's fatal plane crash in summer 1944.

H3: Gefreiter, 5. Gebirgs-Division, 1943

This junior NCO of Gebirgsjäger proudly displays on his left sleeve the *Kreta* cuffband commemorating his service during the hard-fought invasion of Crete in May 1941. On the left side of his Bergmütze, just ahead of the Mountain Troops' regulation Edelweiss badge, is pinned the 'Gams' – the semi-official divisional badge adopted by 5. Gebirgs-Division, in the shape of a small white metal chamois on a mountain peak. His tunic is the M1943 Feldbluse, with plain field-grey collar and subdued collar patches; Waffenfarbe piping appears only around the field-grey shoulder straps. Both the rankers on this plate wear conventional black leather equipment and carry the 98K rifle.

Gebirgsjäger relaxing – cf Plate H. Note the Edelweiss sleeve patch, and the metal badge worn on the side of the Bergmütze. (Ian Jewison)

INDEX